Contents

Chapter 1.
Introduction

"They took K.M., who is 12 years old, in the open air. Her father was killed by the Janjawid in Um Baru, the rest of the family ran away and she was captured by the Janjawid who were on horseback. More than six people used her as a wife; she stayed with the Janjawid and the military more than 10 days. K., another woman who is married, aged 18, ran away but was captured by the Janjawid who slept with her in the open place, all of them slept with her. She is still with them. A., a teacher, told me that they broke her leg after raping her."

A 66-year-old farmer from Um Baru in the district of Kutum, Darfur, western Sudan.[1]

As conflict escalated in late 2003 and early 2004 in Darfur region, western Sudan, Amnesty International began to receive hundreds of reports of rape and other sexual violence against women and girls. It also emerged that women and girls were being abducted to be used as sex slaves or domestic workers.

Most of the perpetrators were members of the government-backed armed militia, the *Janjawid*, but mounting evidence indicated that government soldiers were also involved. Even women who reached refugee camps were not safe. In March 2004 alone, the UN was told that in the camp for internally displaced persons in Mornei, western Darfur, up to 16 women were being raped every day as they went to collect water. The women had to go to the river – their families needed the water and they feared that the men would be killed if they went instead.[2]

A woman prepares food in a camp for displaced people in Erengeti, Democratic Republic of Congo, in July 2003. Thousands of women in the eastern part of the country have been forced to flee their homes through fear of being killed or raped.

The horrific pattern of sexual and other violence against women which has emerged from Darfur is by no means unique. In recent years, hundreds of thousands of women affected by conflict around the world have suffered the same fate. In the recent conflict in the Democratic Republic of Congo (DRC), tens of thousands of women and girls have been raped. In Colombia, widespread sexual violence is an integral part of the armed conflict and is committed by all sides – the security forces, army-backed paramilitaries and guerrilla forces. Lesser known conflicts such as that in the Solomon Islands have also left a legacy of violence against women: in the first six months of 2004 alone, 200 women reported to the Solomon Islands police that they had been raped.[3]

This report attempts to explore some of the underlying reasons for this violence. Evidence gathered by Amnesty International in recent years supports the view that conflict reinforces and exacerbates existing patterns of discrimination and violence against women. The violence women suffer in conflict is an extreme manifestation of the discrimination and abuse women face in peacetime, and the unequal power relations between men and women in most societies. In peacetime, such attitudes contribute to the widespread acceptance of domestic violence, rape and other forms of sexual abuse against women. When political tensions and increasing militarization spill over into outright conflict, these habitual attitudes and abuses take on new dimensions and distinctive patterns, and all forms of violence increase, including rape and other forms of sexual violence against women.

A broad spectrum of violence against women

Although the UN Security Council has recently recognized that "civilians, particularly women and children, account for the vast majority of those adversely affected by armed conflict, including as refugees and internally displaced persons, and increasingly are targeted by combatants and armed elements",[4] there is still a widespread perception that women play only a secondary or peripheral role in situations of conflict.

This report describes the use by states and armed groups of gender-based violence in conflict. The use of rape as a weapon of war is perhaps the most notorious and brutal way in which conflict impacts on women. As rape and sexual violence are so pervasive within situations of conflict, the "rape victim" has become an emblematic image of women's experience of war.

This report seeks to show the many other ways in which women and girls are targeted for violence, or otherwise affected by war, in disproportionate or different ways from men. The report highlights how the many roles which women play in conflict, and the variety of contexts they find themselves in, can have a devastating impact on their physical integrity and basic rights. This report also refers to the broader phenomenon of militarization which often precedes conflict, which almost always accompanies it, and which can remain as part of its legacy. For the purposes of this report, militarization is the process whereby military values, institutions and patterns of behaviour have an increasingly dominant influence over society.

Article 1 of the UN Declaration on the Elimination of Violence against Women states that: *"The term 'violence against women' means any act of gender-based violence that results in, or is likely to result in, physical, sexual or psychological harm or suffering to women, including threats of such acts, coercion or arbitrary deprivation of liberty, whether occurring in public or in private life."*[5]

According to the UN Committee on the Elimination of Discrimination against Women, gender-based violence against women is violence "directed against a woman because she is a woman or that affects women disproportionately."[6]

Women are likely to be among the primary victims of direct attacks on the civilian population, as they usually constitute the majority of the non-combatant population. They also generally bear the brunt of so-called "collateral damage" –

the killing or maiming of civilians as a result of military attacks. Even so-called "precision bombing" exacts a heavy civilian toll, while landmines and unexploded ordnance do not distinguish between military and civilian footsteps. Domestic work, social restrictions on their mobility and other factors may mean that women are often less able to flee when the civilian population comes under attack.

Individual women may be specifically targeted for torture or for killings because they are community leaders, because they have challenged social mores about appropriate roles for women, or because of the activities of their male relatives. Women are targeted as peace activists, as mediators and negotiators in conflict and as human rights defenders and humanitarian aid workers. Many of these abuses take gender-specific forms.

If detained or imprisoned, women may be held in inappropriate detention facilities and will often be at risk of gender-based torture, including rape and other forms of sexual abuse, by their jailors or fellow inmates.

In situations of inter-communal strife or conflicts drawn along ethnic or religious lines, women of a particular community or social group may be assaulted because they are seen as embodying the "honour" and integrity of the community.

Women and children form the majority of the millions of refugees and displaced people fleeing situations of conflict, exposing them to privations of many kinds and to further risk of sexual violence. It has been estimated that 80 per cent of refugees are women and children.[7] Yet refugee camps are often planned and administered in such a way that women living there face discrimination and continued risk of sexual abuse.

The trafficking of women and girls for sexual exploitation and forced labour has been a common characteristic of conflicts and post-conflict situations throughout history. In recent years, UN and other peacekeeping forces, as well as humanitarian aid workers, have been implicated in trafficking.

In many parts of the world, more and more women and girls are becoming combatants, whether voluntarily or by coercion, in both regular armies and armed groups. Some are recruited into armed groups for the purpose of sexual exploitation or are subjected to sexual violence as part of "initiation" rituals. Some also become perpetrators, responsible for human rights abuses. Many other women may be forced to contribute to the war effort in other ways, such as preparing munitions, uniforms and other military equipment.

The increasing international focus on sexual violence committed in the context of conflict, while necessary and important, has tended to obscure other important aspects of women's experience of conflict and militarization. These include the

disproportionate and differential impact of conflict on their economic, social and cultural rights, including their right to health.

An Albanian woman from Kosovo carries her daughter, who had collapsed by the side of the road, into the NATO-organized Radusha refugee camp in Macedonia, controlled by the Macedonian police and army, April 1999. Throughout that year thousands of people fled their homes in Kosovo to escape ethnic violence and NATO bombardment.

The role that women are expected to play as carers and guardians of the family can cause them to be particularly hard hit, both financially and emotionally, by the loss of family members or the destruction of their homes. In conflict situations, many women must take on additional roles as sole heads of household providing for their families. Damage to the economic infrastructure and environment raises particular problems for women in societies where they have primary responsibility for providing food and water for their families. The many women around the world who depend on subsistence agriculture face the risk of crossfire, landmines or forcible eviction. Grazing cattle, tending fields, taking produce to market or collecting water or firewood may prove impossible. War widows have to raise their children while trying to eke out a living in difficult circumstances.

The damage caused by conflict often means that women no longer have access to healthcare appropriate to their needs, whether in their communities, in camps for refugees and displaced people, in prisons, barracks or camps used by combatants, or in demobilization camps established in the aftermath of conflict. When primary healthcare services collapse completely in the context of conflict, women are affected differently, and often disproportionately, because of their distinct health needs and care responsibilities.

In most conflicts, women remain largely absent from peace-making, peacekeeping and peace-building initiatives, even those backed by the international community. In the aftermath of hostilities, disarmament, demobilization, rehabilitation and reintegration programmes may not cater for their needs or match their experiences.

Violence can take a variety of different forms, psychological as well as physical, resulting in extreme economic hardship and social deprivation which deny women economic, social and cultural rights, as well as their civil and political rights. Even where women suffer the same human rights violations as men, these may have different consequences for women. Women often face particular barriers to access to justice and redress, and endure social stigma in post-conflict societies because of the abuses they have suffered.

Those who carry out the abuses are many and varied: soldiers of the state's armed forces; pro-government paramilitary groups or militias; armed groups fighting the government or at war with other armed groups; the police, prison guards or private security and military personnel; military forces stationed abroad, including UN and other peacekeeping forces; staff of humanitarian agencies; neighbours and relatives. Places where such violence occurs are equally diverse: detention centres, displaced persons and refugee camps, at checkpoints and border crossings, in public places, in the community and in the home.

The gender of conflict

The rhetoric, institutions and processes of war and militarization have been described as inherently male-centred, premised on values which prize male aggression and devalue characteristics associated with women. The gender-stereotyping often used in arguments for war has very real consequences for the way conflict is conducted. Women's bodies, their sexuality and reproductive capacity, are often used as a symbolic and literal battleground.

Gender-based discrimination and violence are therefore not incidental to conflict, but are embedded in all aspects of warfare. Violence against women has been an integral and endemic aspect of conflict throughout history. But that does not mean violence against women in war is inevitable or intractable. Patterns of violence against women in conflict do not arise "naturally", but are ordered, condoned or

A family in Rafah (Gaza Strip), sitting in the remnants of their house which was severely damaged by Israeli forces. More than 3,000 homes, vast areas of agricultural land and hundreds of other properties have been destroyed by the Israeli army and security forces in the Occupied Territories of the West Bank and Gaza Strip since September 2000.

tolerated as a result of political calculations. Furthermore, these crimes are committed by individuals who know they will not be punished for attacking women and girls. Stereotypical or violent attitudes to women already prevalent in society are consciously inflamed or manipulated by those forces – military, political, social or economic – which consider that such a strategy of war will be to their advantage.

Men and boys are also targeted for violence, including sexual violence, in conflicts and women can also be perpetrators of abuses, or – as in the case of girl soldiers – both victims and perpetrators simultaneously. However, this report focuses on the impact of conflict-related violence on women and girls as part of Amnesty International's campaign to Stop Violence Against Women. The assumption that wars are fought between largely male armies has led to women being seen merely as part of the backdrop. Men are viewed as the key protagonists and main actors of conflict, while women are seen as only occasional, "collateral" victims. Because of these assumptions, the stories of women are rarely highlighted in histories of conflict. The full and complex dimensions of their experience are rarely covered in depth by the news media. Critically, women's voices have almost always been left out of any process of conflict resolution and post-conflict reconstruction.

Despite its ubiquitous nature, the scale and nature of violence against women in the context of militarization and conflict have been largely ignored by historians, peace-makers and the general public. Women's experiences have been marginalized from the political and human rights agenda in times of emergency or in the aftermath of conflict.

One reason such abuses have remained hidden is the customary separation between the "public" and "private" spheres of life, with so-called private violence against women not seen as a proper realm for action by national and international courts.

Other reasons include the difficulty of prosecuting sexual crimes, a difficulty exacerbated in times of conflict that contributes to the impunity enjoyed by so many perpetrators of sexual violence. Knowing this, many women choose not to report rape. Many women hide or deny the abuse for fear of social stigma, or because their coping mechanisms may dispose them not to publicize or seek redress for the abuses they have suffered. Social stigma is greatly increased by the failure of states to prevent and prosecute sexualized violence, leading women to feel doubly victimized in their attempts to seek justice.

Yet another reason that women's experiences of militarization and conflict have been ignored or overlooked is that women have customarily not been represented in the political, military and international institutions deciding on matters of war and peace. Historically, women have had little participation in efforts to develop the rules of war. For example, of over 240 representatives to the Diplomatic Conference that adopted the Geneva Conventions, only 13 were women.[8] The particular impact of conflict and militarization upon women was therefore little reflected in the rules of war and the international community was slow to recognize violence against women in any context as a human rights issue. It has also been slow to involve women in peace-making, peacekeeping and peace-building operations, or in the aftermath of conflict, in disarmament, demobilization, and reintegration initiatives.

A decade of progress?

Over the last decade there has been significant progress in documenting and publicizing what has happened to women caught in conflict, largely as a result of the determined and courageous work of women's rights activists and advocates.

Significant progress has also been made in recognizing acts of violence against women as gross violations or abuses of international human rights and international humanitarian law, which the international community as a whole has an obligation to address, and as international crimes.

It is now 10 years since the UN Special Rapporteur on violence against women was appointed as a result of the adoption of the UN Declaration on the Elimination of Violence against Women. Mandated to analyze the contexts, causes and consequences of violence against women worldwide, the first two post holders have devoted particular attention to situations of conflict and insecurity.

At the UN's Fourth World Conference on Women in Beijing in 1995, governments gave a renewed commitment to address the widespread prevalence of violence against women in conflict. From the mid-1990s onwards, rape and other forms of sexual violence were increasingly recognized as among the most serious crimes under international law. The landmark judgements of the international tribunals set up to prosecute crimes committed in the conflicts in the former Yugoslavia and Rwanda, as well as in the historic adoption of the Rome Statute of the International Criminal Court in 1998, underscored the gravity of rape and other crimes of sexual violence.

International understanding is also growing at the highest level regarding the vital importance of including women and their experiences in peace processes and post-conflict reconstruction efforts. In 2000, the groundbreaking UN Security Council Resolution 1325 linked the maintenance of international peace and security to the need for full and equal participation of women in all levels of decision-making before conflict breaks out, during hostilities and afterwards. Activists for women's rights were essential to the passage of this resolution, and are now campaigning to see it implemented in practice.

Campaigning and advocacy by women human rights defenders around the world has been instrumental in these achievements at the local, national and international levels. Often against great odds, they have campaigned tirelessly for justice, aimed not just at criminalizing and prosecuting violations against women but at changing the structures of society which marginalize women and make them vulnerable to violence in all settings. They have promoted new visions of security based around the notion of human security, in contrast to state or military security.

Key international agencies involved in humanitarian, human rights and development efforts have made real advances in reviewing the effectiveness and impact of their work to prevent violence and other abuses against women.

The last decade has seen major breakthroughs at the level of international standards, mechanisms and commitments to tackle violence against women. But the shocking scale and stubborn persistence of violence against women in today's ongoing conflicts, as documented by Amnesty International throughout 2004 in countries including Afghanistan, Colombia, the DRC, Sudan and Nepal, suggests that this is not enough.

Ten years on from the genocide in Rwanda, where violence against women was a central element of the strategy to eliminate a particular ethnic group, little or nothing seems to have been learned about how to prevent such horrors. For all the commitments at the international level, effective tools for ending violence against women seem sorely lacking in practice.

Evaluating the progress made 10 years after her post was established, the UN Special Rapporteur on violence against women highlighted the lack of will to implement international standards effectively, the backlash against women's reproductive rights and a changed global security context as key challenges in the struggle to end violence against women.[9]

Conflict and security in the 21st century

Military aggression, foreign occupation, failed or collapsed states, inter-communal tensions or conflicts generated by competition for resources are an ongoing reality affecting people across the globe. The number of conflicts shows no signs of waning. Between 1989 and 1997 for example, there were an estimated 103 armed conflicts in 69 countries.[10] In Africa alone, over one quarter of the continent's 53 countries suffered conflicts in the late 1990s.[11] And in this world at war, the victims are increasingly civilians, most of whom are non-combatant women and children.[12]

A common characteristic of many conflicts at the start of the 21st century is the exploitation of perceived racial, ethnic, religious, cultural or political differences in order to set community against community. In such contexts, sexual violence is particularly likely to be used as a weapon of war. Women of a particular racial, ethnic or religious group may be targeted for violence aimed at their sexual integrity and reproductive capacity, as the perceived bearers of the community's cultural identity and the reproducers of their society.

Few of today's wars are international conflicts fought exclusively between professional national armies. Although international tensions continue in numerous parts of the world, the majority of conflicts are internal conflicts between governments and armed groups, or between several competing armed groups. Some of the worst atrocities against women have been committed by "non-state actors", in particular by armed groups.[13] Holding those responsible to account can be a formidable challenge. The chain-of-command structure of such

Participants in AI Nepal's Stop Violence Against Women campaign launch rally in Banepa, near Kathmandu, March 2004. Amnesty International members were joined by women activists from other non-governmental organizations.

groups may be difficult to establish. They may not recognize any obligations under international humanitarian law. Judicial mechanisms for bringing the perpetrators to justice in accordance with fair trial standards may not exist, particularly in areas under armed group control.

The devastating attacks on 11 September 2001 highlighted a new type of threat from armed groups. While acts of terror against civilians are nothing new, attacks such as those in Nairobi, New York, Bali, Casablanca, Madrid and Beslan shocked the conscience of people worldwide because of their scale and deliberate cruelty. The fact that many of today's armed groups operate in loose international networks using such tactics as suicide bombing makes it all the more difficult to track down those responsible and prevent future attacks.

The new global security environment since 11 September 2001 has led to abuses by governments in the context of the US-led "war on terror". New doctrines of security have stretched the concept of "war" into areas formerly considered law enforcement, promoting the notion that human rights can be curtailed when it comes to the detention, interrogation and prosecution of "terrorist" suspects.

The new security environment has also led to some countries imposing greater restrictions on immigrants and asylum-seekers, many of them women who have fled conflict or who sought to work and send funds back to family members in war-torn countries. For example, the effect of procedural delays and limitations imposed by the US government after 11 September 2001 led to a sharp fall in the number of foreigners who became permanent US immigrants in 2003.[14] Increased restrictions on would-be refugees, migrant workers or immigrants have also been reported from other countries including Japan, where restrictions are likely to impact particularly on women domestic workers seeking employment there.

The US-led military intervention in Iraq has heightened concerns that the world may be entering a new era of preventive or pre-emptive wars, where military force may be used in disregard of the restrictions contained in the UN Charter. Given the prominent position of the USA on the world stage, US policy will to a great extent determine future trends regarding militarization, the use of force and the conduct of armed conflict.

Another characteristic of contemporary conflict is the role of powerful economic interests in fanning the flames and reaping the profits of conflict and militarization. If more conflicts are fought over natural resources in future, the role of corporate actors will be all the more significant and decisive. Just as women's experiences can no longer be overlooked in policy debates around security, so urgent attention will need to be paid to the economic and social dimensions of human security if future conflicts are to be averted.

Amnesty International's campaign: a call to action

Today, there can no longer be any excuse for ignoring the scale of crimes against women in conflict. With almost daily news reports from war zones across the globe, no one can claim that they do not know what is happening. Nor can one hide behind the excuse that nothing can be done. There is an urgent need to find more effective forms of action proportionate to the scale and gravity of the crimes that are unfolding.

This report is not intended as a catalogue of horrors, but as a call to action. Amnesty International has launched a long-term worldwide campaign to Stop

A player at a Turkish football match. Both teams wore Stop Violence Against Women T-shirts, February 2004. On the front of the T-shirts is the slogan 'Red Card for violence against women'.

Violence Against Women. One of its aims is to show the continuum of violence against women, from peace to war, from the home to public spaces. The campaign includes a focus on the prevention of violence against women in conflict-related situations. To this end Amnesty International is presenting an agenda for action at the global, regional, national and local level, setting out concrete steps that can be taken to challenge violence against women, to support survivors and human rights defenders working with them, and to bring about a world in which women can enjoy peace and security in all spheres of their lives.

Ending violence against women is an ambitious goal, but Amnesty International believes that a massive and coordinated mobilization of individuals, organizations and institutions around the world can bring it within reach. Amnesty International is proposing an agenda for change around which it hopes a range of actors will converge, including political figures, non-governmental organizations, the media and ordinary people, men as well as women.

Amnesty International's agenda centres around the need to prevent or stop violence against women, bring to justice those who carry it out, provide redress to survivors and promote women's role in processes affecting their lives. It draws on and complements the work of other organizations long active in this field around the world.

Amnesty International believes these are essential steps towards a future where women will no longer be objects of war but subjects of peace, no longer victims of abuse but bearers of rights. This future is in our hands.

Scope and methodology of this report

Sources

The findings of this report are based on Amnesty International's research and campaigning on numerous situations of conflict and collective violence around the world over the last decade, as well as the organization's involvement in advocacy and standard-setting at the international level. They also draw on the research and analysis of academics, journalists and women's rights advocates working on violence against women in armed conflict worldwide. The report is part of a series of publications issued by Amnesty International as part of its campaign to Stop Violence Against Women.[15]

Many of the testimonies and cases cited do not name the victims or survivors, or give exact biographical details. In most cases this is to protect the identity of the women and girls concerned and to respect their security and that of their relatives. It is worth noting, however, that Amnesty International has found that many survivors of violence against women – when offered the right circumstances such as assurances about privacy, confidentiality and gender-sensitive, preferably female, interviewers – will courageously tell their stories in order to help bring perpetrators to justice and prevent other women from having to experience what they went through.

Conflict and militarization: a continuum of violence

This report is based on the recognition that armed conflict is part of a broader continuum of collective violence.[16] Most examples in the report are drawn from situations of armed conflict, whether international (between the armies of different states) or non-international (between state and armed opposition forces, or involving several warring armed groups). But the report also addresses other situations of collective violence, including inter-communal violence, which may not amount to armed conflict under international humanitarian law. It also covers pre-

and post-conflict situations in recognition of the importance of addressing gender-based violence in situations of impending conflict as well as in their aftermath.

International humanitarian law distinguishes between "armed conflicts" and "situations of internal disturbances and tensions, such as riots, isolated and sporadic acts of violence and other acts of a similar nature" which fall below the threshold of armed conflict and to which humanitarian law does not apply.[17]

It is often difficult to draw clear-cut distinctions between different types of armed conflict or collective violence. Such distinctions, based on the intensity of the violence and the international or non-international nature of the conflict, may appear irrelevant on the ground, where people are suffering irrespective of such categories. Yet these distinctions have implications for the body of applicable international law and so need to be taken into account in efforts to get warring parties to respect the fundamental rules and principles of humanity in any given situation.

It can also be difficult to define and determine precisely when pre-conflict conditions become armed conflict, or to agree exactly when conflict has definitely ended and evolves into a post-conflict phase. Such determinations may be highly politicized or partial, and some post-conflict situations contain the seeds for new or renewed conflict.

The increased use of force to resolve international and internal disputes, the proliferation of arms and the vilification and dehumanization of the "enemy", whether internal or external, can all be seen as characteristics of a broader phenomenon of militarization within a society. A similar process may be observed on a global level, with the dramatic rise in global military expenditure and the subordination of human rights concerns to a narrowly defined "security" agenda.[18]

The focus of this report is not intended to suggest that violence against women is confined to situations of armed conflict. For women and girls, both peace and war can be times of discrimination and violence. Amnesty International's work has addressed gender-based violence in the home, in the community and in the custody of the state, and has highlighted how violence against women occurs across a broad spectrum of interrelated contexts.[19]

For the purposes of this report, the term "conflict" is used to include communal conflicts, disturbances and other situations which may not amount to an armed conflict under international humanitarian law. The report also addresses militarization, pre-conflict and post-conflict situations. The relevant laws therefore span international law as it applies to peacetime; to situations of disturbances, tensions and similar low-level clashes not amounting to armed conflict; and to the full range of armed conflicts.

Four subsets of international law are relevant: international human rights law; refugee law; international humanitarian law; and international criminal law. All comprise both treaties and rules of general, or customary, international law. A number of regional legal instruments and mechanisms for the protection of human rights have also been significant in addressing violence against women. (See the Appendix for a list of the main relevant international and regional treaties and standards.)

Violence against women: a range of rights abuses

Gender-based violence is both physical and psychological, and can entail a constellation of human rights violations. Not all forms of harm suffered by women in conflict necessarily fall under the definition of violence against women or constitute unlawful acts under international human rights or humanitarian law. For example, the killing of a woman combatant in the course of armed confrontation is not in itself unlawful, nor covered by the definition in the UN Declaration on the Elimination of Violence against Women. In this report, Amnesty International refers to violence against women which is in some way gender-based because it can be said to have gender-specific causes, manifestations or consequences, and which is in violation of applicable international standards.

In looking at violence against women in conflict, it is important to recognize that the experience of individual women will be influenced by their particular political and cultural context and by aspects of their identity, beliefs and situation in society. Discrimination on such grounds as race, ethnicity, religion, sexual orientation, class or economic status can compound the risk of gender-based violence that certain women face. It can also hamper their access to justice and redress. As Radhika Coomaraswamy, the first UN Special Rapporteur on violence against women, has documented, the effects of racism, xenophobia and other forms of prejudice can further undermine the security of migrant, indigenous, minority and other marginalized women around the world in situations of conflict and internal tension.[20]

Chapter 2.
Gender, violence and conflict

The factors which contribute to violence against women in situations of conflict and militarization have their roots in the pervasive discrimination women face in peacetime as well as during and after conflict. Violence and discrimination against women are embedded in the language and rhetoric of conflict and militarization. They appear to be an inherent feature of the conduct of war and endemic in the institutions waging it.

In peacetime women rarely have the same economic resources, political rights, authority or control over their environment and needs as men. Situations of armed conflict typically exacerbate women's unequal status in society, fuelling the conditions for even greater discrimination and violence against them.

Conflict and militarization reinforce sexist stereotyping and rigid differentiation of gender roles. Weapons proliferate and violence becomes an everyday means of social interaction. Conflict often creates conditions of severe economic deprivation where the civilian population – and in particular women – becomes almost totally dependent on certain authorities (whether occupation forces, peacekeepers or humanitarian workers) for survival, leaving them acutely vulnerable to sexual and other forms of exploitation. In emergency situations civil or political rights are suspended in law or in practice, which further restricts women's ability to challenge or influence the course of events around them.

A Sierra Leonean survivor of amputation caring for her baby, 2001. In a decade of internal armed conflict in Sierra Leone, many thousands of civilians, including children, were raped, abducted, forcibly recruited to fight, mutilated and killed. Mutilation by the deliberate cutting off of limbs was commonplace. More than 90 per cent of women and girls abducted by armed opposition forces during the prolonged conflict are believed to have been raped.

There are many other gender-specific impacts of militarization on women's security. Before a shot has been fired, increased militarization and diversion of resources into armaments often impacts most negatively on women, as healthcare, maternity benefits, childcare and education for both children and women are downgraded or set aside as secondary to "national security issues". UNIFEM has, for example, pointed out that the cost of funding an F-22 fighter plane could pay the annual healthcare expenses for 1.3 million women in the USA.[21] In January 2003, US President George Bush announced he was planning to ask Congress to commit US$15 billion over the next five years to halt the spread of AIDS. At around the same time, military and surveillance activities in Central Asia as part of the US "war on terror" were costing US$2 billion a month.[22]

Gender is also central to the debate about the legality and ethics of military intervention, including the use of force against another state, in the name of human rights. This debate has intensified in the light of military intervention in Afghanistan and Iraq, and the ongoing human rights crisis in Darfur, western Sudan.

There are particularly dire consequences for women when intervention does not occur to stop gross human rights abuses, as in the former Yugoslavia and Rwanda in the 1990s. But there are also grave consequences for women when armed intervention does occur, as trafficking in women and girls, forced prostitution, and other gender-based violence often become rampant in such contexts. Some feminist scholars have suggested that states may be reluctant to intervene with force when all that is seen to be at stake are women's lives and bodies.[23] Others point to the selective use of concern for women's human rights as a reason for intervention, for example in Afghanistan.

Gender-based violence affects not only women and girls, but also men and boys. In many conflicts, men are more likely to be killed, while women are more likely to suffer sexual violence. However, men have also been subjected to sexual violence in war. In the former Yugoslavia, for example, men were forced to sexually abuse other men while being mocked by their captors. US occupation forces have used similar techniques during interrogation of Iraqi detainees following the occupation of Iraq in 2003. In the DRC, young boys and men are raped as a means of reprisal against individuals, families or communities, and to undermine the fundamental values and social fabric of the community. Like women, men who have suffered sexual violence face social stigma, which, like women, often influences their decision on whether or not to pursue justice.

Words and deeds: rhetoric and gender-based violence

Throughout history and across cultures, gender-based violence has featured heavily in the rhetoric used by government officials, religious and community leaders, and armed groups to mobilize hostile and often dehumanizing attitudes towards the enemy in times of impending conflict. This rhetoric can contribute to a cycle of escalating violence.

Wartime propaganda in many countries has illustrated how gender stereotypes are strengthened in the lead-up to and during conflict, to bolster military forces, to undermine opponents and to ensure that women will play the necessary "feminine" war support roles. At the heart of this rhetoric is the notion that women – and in particular women's bodies, sexuality and reproductive capacity – are the repositories of the community's honour. Imagery involving the rape of women is commonly used to strengthen the sense of communal solidarity and increase fear and distrust of the "enemy". In Europe during the Second World War, for example, scare stories were spread on both sides about the rape of women by the enemy. Posters in France portrayed the rape of "Marianne", the symbol of France, evoking the fear of the actual rape of French women and the symbolic rape of the nation.

Similarly, in the Indian state of Gujarat, a distorted history was used to promote the myth and imagery of the virile, violent Muslim man and the victimized Hindu woman. Hindu women purportedly in danger of rape were conflated with "Mother India", and the fictionalized history of the rape of both became the justification for the rape of Muslim women. There was little doubt that such hate propaganda contributed to widespread sexual abuse of Muslim women during inter-communal violence in February 2002.[24]

Inherent in much of the sexualized and gender-based rhetoric so prevalent before and during conflict is a clear incitement to violence against women. As a result, sexual violence often becomes an intentional strategy to terrorize, demean and "defeat" an entire population, as well as a way of engendering hatred and destruction. An attack on women can be seen as an attack on the entire community – an affront not only to the women assaulted but also to those who should have protected them. Victory over an enemy force can be interpreted as a licence to rape, with women's bodies seen as the spoils of war. Throughout history women's bodies have been considered the legitimate booty of victorious armies. Tacit or explicit licence to rape is given by commanders as a means of "bonding" the men in their units.

Attacks on women are sometimes directed against them as the "carrier" of the next generation of the "enemy". This explains why attacks on women sometimes include mutilation of their genitalia or the cutting out and destruction of foetuses. During the armed conflict in Guatemala, for example, which lasted for more than three decades with varying intensity from the 1960s, soldiers told Amnesty International that they had carried out such acts to "eliminate guerrilla spawn".[25]

Similar atrocities were reported in 2004 in Sudan and during recent conflicts in a number of other countries in Africa, where women's genitalia were mutilated after rape or displayed as trophies of war.

Approaching conflict makes a community more intent on preserving what it sees as intrinsic to its national, religious or cultural identity. Propaganda and social pressures may focus on the expectation that women will "breed soldiers". Inter-ethnic marriages may be banned and there may be increased control exercised over women's sexuality, the way they dress, their freedom of movement or their activities outside the home.

Given that ideals of women's sexual purity and integrity are commonly cited in the rhetoric of conflict, and are used in attempts to differentiate the enemy group, women who are seen as departing from rigid sexual "norms" and stereotypes are frequently attacked for betraying the culture and identity of the community. This is especially true of lesbian and bisexual women, who may be at risk of even more violent forms of discrimination than in peacetime.[26]

Homosexuality is often portrayed as a characteristic of the enemy – "unpatriotic", "unrevolutionary" or a "foreign import". Lesbian women, along with gay men, bisexuals and transgender people have been assaulted as a result.

Amnesty International research in Colombia in 2004 found that in militarized communities where the army, army-backed paramilitary forces and guerrilla groups have a presence, gender stereotyping is exacerbated, increasing the risk of gender-based violence against those thought to be lesbian, gay or bisexual. In late 2002, in the city of Medellín, a 14-year-old girl was stripped in the street and a sign saying "I am a lesbian" was hung around her neck. According to witnesses, she was then raped by three men. Her body was found days later; her breasts had been cut off.[27] There have also been reports in Colombia of paramilitary forces and guerrilla groups attacking lesbians, bisexuals, gay men or people suspected of having HIV/AIDS.

The military: a gender-based culture

Social attitudes alone do not explain the increased violence against women in conflict. The very ethos and values inscribed in military institutions often encourage violence against women. The culture of armed forces is generally premised on male stereotypes, prizing aggression and devaluing attributes traditionally associated with women. Armies extol, encourage and enforce male bonding and expressions of virility so that soldiers trust each other, are less ready to display weakness in front of their peers, and become more willing to take the risks that make them a good fighting unit.[28]

Many analysts have highlighted the profoundly "gendered" nature of military organization. Military structures are seen as perpetuating gender stereotypes of the "strong male" army protecting the "weak female" civilian population.[29]

Such values are reinforced by the overwhelmingly male composition of armed forces around the world. There are 23 million soldiers in standing armies around the world, of whom some 97 per cent are male. Women serving in armed forces tend to be in administrative or "caring" roles. Combat forces have been estimated as being 99 per cent male.[30] The fact that very few states allow women to hold posts that might directly involve combat is a reflection of the widespread notion that women are intrinsically unsuited to such activity. A number of states have made reservations to the Convention on the Elimination of All Forms of Discrimination against Women arguing that the principle of equality in public life does not extend to combat-related duties.

Equally striking is the fact that women involved in the armed forces have themselves been perpetrators of sexual abuses or harassment against men, as the images of US women soldiers taunting and ill-treating Iraqi detainees attest. This suggests that merely recruiting women into armed forces will not in itself be sufficient to change their institutional values and ethos.

For some women, involvement in the war effort, whether as combatants in state armies or armed groups, or as civilians, has had some positive benefits.[31] War has presented some women with the opportunity to enter the labour market, gaining certain freedoms and enjoying a new status. Women's participation in nationalist and revolutionary struggles has sometimes facilitated their subsequent assertion of political rights. However, it is often difficult for women to retain these benefits after the conflict is over, and the disruption in traditional gender roles is itself linked to the high incidence of domestic violence in conflict and post-conflict situations.

The contexts in which armed forces operate also foster attitudes conducive to violence against women. In situations of military occupation, for example, male soldiers are removed from their communities, homes, partners and families, and at the same time are often surrounded by a civilian population, mostly made up of women, which is seen as the enemy or as inferior, racially or otherwise. The extra resources often at the disposal of an occupying army and the destitution of many women in conflict and post-conflict situations can facilitate sexual violence and exploitation of women.

During the US war against Viet Nam in the 1960s and 1970s, the killing of Vietnamese civilians and the destruction of entire villages became known via television coverage. Less well known was the extent to which US troops attacked Vietnamese women, which they reportedly saw as a way of humiliating Vietnamese men. US soldiers in Viet Nam reportedly gained the status of "double veteran" by first forcing themselves sexually on a woman, either singly or with "buddies" in gang rapes, and then by murdering the victim.[32]

Trafficking of women on a large scale for prostitution has been a feature of wars and other military operations for centuries. During World War II, some 200,000 women from across Asia were forced into sexual slavery in so-called "comfort stations" by the Japanese Imperial Army.

In recent years, regular armed forces, armed opposition groups, militias, humanitarian workers and international peacekeepers have all been involved in trafficking women for sexual exploitation. The trafficking of girls as young as 12 has grown into a massive industry in the Balkans, for example, fuelled by the demand for the services of prostitutes by members of international forces stationed there. Some troops serving with KFOR, the NATO-led international

Chechen civilians in Grozny during a lull in the fighting in August 1996. Since the collapse of the Soviet Union in 1991, Chechnya has suffered two armed conflicts – 1994 to 1996, and September 1999 to the present. Both have been characterized by reports of indiscriminate attacks on densely populated, residential areas and widespread serious human rights violations by Russian Federation forces, as well as by gross human rights abuses by Chechen forces.

peacekeeping force in Kosovo, have been suspected of involvement in the trafficking of women into forced prostitution. They are, however, immune from prosecution in Kosovo unless their battalion commander waives that immunity.[33] No prosecutions for involvement in trafficking are known to have been initiated by their home countries.[34]

Women and girls are not only trafficked for prostitution. They are also trafficked to provide forced labour, for example in agriculture or as domestic workers. In Cambodia, for example, women who have lost limbs or been disfigured by landmines, as well as elderly women, have been trafficked to Thailand in order to work as beggars.[35]

The legacy of conflict

It is not just the means and methods of warfare that result in violence against women. The political and economic context of conflict, the processes and arguments leading up to it, the military institutions involved and the values they embody, the environment it creates and the legacy it leaves can all fuel discrimination and violence against women.

All these factors can remain long after a conflict has formally ended. Alarming levels of violence against women have surfaced as a major concern in post-conflict situations in Central America, where a spate of gender-based killings in the community and family has been linked in various ways to the legacy of the conflict which ravaged the region up until the mid-1990s. While few have been effectively investigated, these crimes have been attributed to a combination of factors, including the economic and social problems associated with the winding down of the war economy, the demobilization of combatants, the prevalence of small arms and other weapons, an entrenched climate of impunity and the shifts in gender relations in the conflict and post-conflict years.[36]

Increased domestic violence has also been reported in the aftermath of other conflicts. The reasons include the generalized climate of violence which leads to increased resort to force in social relations, the widespread trauma experienced by conflict survivors, the frustrations generated by lack of jobs, shelter and basic services, and the tensions accompanying shifts in traditional gender roles within the family.[37]

In the Occupied Territories of Gaza and the West Bank, for example, Palestinian women have suffered increased levels of domestic violence – alongside the violence of the destruction of their homes, communities and livelihoods by Israeli forces – since the *intifada* (uprising) began in 2000.[38] Many Palestinian institutions have observed that domestic violence has increased in line with rises in the level of violence outside the home.[39] Palestinian women have reported that some men who had been detained by Israeli forces were inflicting ill-treatment on their wives, mirroring the interrogation methods which they had suffered themselves in prison.[40]

In the USA, soldiers and former soldiers figure disproportionately as perpetrators in statistics of violence against female family members, a fact attributed to the authoritarianism inculcated in the military, the customary use of force in training, and the stress produced by perpetual moves and separations.[41] In 1996, a study by the Pentagon found that from 1991 to 1995, more than 50,000 active-duty service members had hit or physically hurt their spouses.[42] Within a six-week period in 2002, four women were killed by their husbands, members of the US Special Forces, at the Fort Bragg military base, North Carolina. Three of the men had just returned from serving as special operations troops in Afghanistan.

Afghanistan

'We have complained but no one listens to us'

Despite the formal cessation of hostilities and the establishment of an interim government in Afghanistan, various armed groups continue to control large parts of the country. Women and girls continue to be threatened with violence in many aspects of their life, both private and public. The disarmament and demobilization process has made progress, albeit slowly, but weapons remain a mainstay of Afghan men's lives. Violence against women and girls, including rape, mental and physical cruelty, forced marriages and exchange of girls to settle disputes are widespread. Institutions for the protection of human rights and the implementation of the rule of law remain weak. As a consequence, a climate of impunity prevails, enjoyed by armed groups across Afghanistan. In the absence of protection and justice, women remain extremely vulnerable.

A 20-year-old woman from the central highlands of Afghanistan was raped in the vicinity of her village by a local armed faction leader. She told Amnesty International:

"I'm suffering from what happened to me. I was washing dishes in the spring well close to my home. I felt a touch on my shoulder, turned around and saw it was the local commander of the village. He grabbed me, threw me on the ground and raped me. The whole village could hear my screams, saw what was happening to me but would not help me. My father-in-law and three brothers-in-law came running to help me and were beaten and threatened by the commander and his men. They were released but the commander told them he would not touch them now but that he would make sure he would kill them. We left that same night and walked through the mountains to Kabul. Many women in this district have been raped by this man and his brother. He has been commander of this area for four years and many families have left because of his violence, looting and killing...

"For many years we have complained but no one listens to us. We have complained to the authorities and many others. The authorities cannot do anything in our area as the commander is the one who is the authority."

At least a dozen women claim that they have been raped by members of armed groups in the central highlands. Amnesty International has received reports that more than 50 families have moved from there to Kabul, claming persecution, intimidation and sexual violence by certain leaders of armed groups.

Chapter 3.
Rape as a weapon of war

As a weapon of war, rape is used strategically and tactically to advance specific objectives in many forms of conflict. It is used to conquer, expel or control women and their communities in times of war or internal conflict. As a form of gender-based torture it is used to extract information, punish, intimidate and humiliate. It is the universal weapon employed to strip women of their dignity and destroy their sense of self. It is also used to terrorize and destroy entire communities. Sometimes rape is committed by all parties to a conflict. But in some conflicts, Amnesty International has found evidence that rape is overwhelmingly committed by one side against the other.

Rape as part of an attack on a community

In some acts of collective violence, rape is used systematically and deliberately to drive out one group of people and empty the land of its settled population. The attack may be highly gendered – while men are killed, women are subjected to rape and other forms of sexual assault.

Women are attacked to destroy their mental and physical integrity. They are attacked publicly to demonstrate the powerlessness of men to defend the community. And they are attacked as bearers of the next generation – their reproductive capacity is either destroyed or harnessed through forcible impregnation to carry the child of the enemy.

Rape as part of an attack on a community can be an element of genocide. When killings and other crimes, including rape, are committed with intent to destroy in whole or in part, a national, ethnic, racial or religious group, whether in peace or war, then the crimes constitute genocide.

In the case of Jean-Paul Akayesu, mayor of Taba commune in Rwanda, who was tried by the International Criminal Tribunal for Rwanda in 1998, the tribunal determined that rapes were part of the genocidal attack.[43] Jean-Paul Akayesu was accused of inciting and ordering the murder, torture and rape of Tutsis who sought refuge in the commune during the 1994 genocide. He was convicted of committing torture himself, and was convicted of murder and rape through ordering and otherwise aiding and abetting those crimes.

Rape of women in custody

Amnesty International's long-term work on prisoners has shown that some forms of torture or ill-treatment – such as rape, sexual mutilation, sexual humiliation, threats of rape, and verbal abuse of a sexual nature – are more consistently directed at women detainees. Other forms of torture can only be inflicted on women. Forms of gender-specific torture or ill-treatment reported by Amnesty International include: pregnant prisoners being given electric shocks; medical care being withheld leading to miscarriages; body searches and forced vaginal examinations; and objects being inserted into women's vaginas.

Women and girls in detention during conflict are highly vulnerable. Women and girls may be detained because of their suspected opposition to the government of the day; their activities as human rights defenders or as journalists reporting on conflicts or government policies; their membership of a particular ethnic, religious or racial group; or simply because of their relationship to men considered "subversive" or anti-government.

Eighteen-year-old Reena Rasaili was detained by security forces in Pokhari village, Kavre district, in Nepal in February 2004. Witnesses said that about 20 men in plain clothes arrived at her home at midnight. They broke down the door and about 10 men went in. They questioned the family, searched the house, and took Reena outside to interrogate her about Communist Party of Nepal (CPN) (Maoist) activities in the village. An officer then ordered five of his men to take her to a cowshed near the house. At 5am Reena Rasaili was taken to a spot about 100 metres from her house. Three shots were then heard. Villagers found her naked body after the security forces left the village. There were bloodstains on her discarded clothes and underwear, suggesting that she had been raped before she was killed.

Sudan

Rape as part of a widespread and systematic attack

The current humanitarian crisis in the western Sudanese state of Darfur began in 2003 when insurgents founded two armed political groups, although the region had already been under a state of emergency for two years. The Sudanese government responded to the insurgency by supporting and arming militia known as the *Janjawid*, or "men on horseback". These mostly nomadic militiamen started a campaign targeted at the African agro-pastoralist groups living in Darfur and suspected of supporting the armed groups. Since then, at least 1.4 million people have been forced from their homes, both within Darfur and into neighbouring Chad.

Tens of thousands of men and women have been killed, thousands of women raped and more than a million villagers forcibly displaced from their homes which have then been burned down. Their crops and cattle, their main means of subsistence, have been looted or destroyed. These human rights violations have been committed in a systematic manner by the *Janjawid*, often in coordination with Sudanese soldiers and the Sudanese Air Force.

The violence inflicted on the civilian population has been highly gender-based. Men have been taken away and then executed by the *Janjawid*; women have been systematically raped. Women who tried to escape from villages have been shot.

Women in Darfur are more accessible to aggressors during attacks, because they usually stay closer to the village, compared with men who tend to herd cattle further away from the village. They are responsible for caring for children and other family dependants, leaving them more vulnerable during attacks and flight.

In many cases, women have been publicly raped, in front of their husbands, relatives or the wider community. Pregnant women have not been spared. Those who have resisted rapes were reportedly beaten, stabbed or killed.

Women and girls as young as eight years old have been abducted during attacks and forced to stay with the *Janjawid* in military camps or hideouts. Several testimonies collected by Amnesty International contain clear cases of sexual slavery; some record women and girls' legs and arms being deliberately broken to prevent them from escaping.

Women who have succeeded in finding their way to a camp for refugees or the internally displaced still risk attack. The internally displaced population, who have largely gathered at the periphery of the towns and large villages of the region, are restricted in their movement by *Janjawid* groups who patrol outside the camps and settlements. Men do not leave the settlements for fear of being killed; women who have ventured outside the camps in order to fetch desperately needed wood, food or water have been raped and harassed.

Women are often reluctant to report rape to medical workers, which can lead to further complications of their injuries. One factor contributing to this reluctance is a legal requirement that all cases of rape be reported to the police before medical workers can give survivors treatment, which has only recently been rescinded. The Minister of Justice sent out a decree to change this (dated 21 August 2004), but it had not been communicated to Darfur health authorities at the time of an Amnesty International visit to the area weeks later.

The strong cultural, social and religious taboos against rape in Darfur also make it harder for women to speak out. Amnesty International has been told by Sudanese officials that these traditions mean that widespread rape could not have occurred in Darfur. The government of Sudan has denied that widespread sexual violence has been perpetrated in Darfur, one of the factors behind the lack of commitment from the police and judiciary to investigate these cases.

At present there are not enough trained medical workers to identify and treat survivors of rape in Darfur. There are also insufficient medical facilities to treat sexually transmitted diseases spread through rape. Women who become pregnant as a result of rape are likely to suffer further abuses of their rights. There is the trauma of the rape itself as well as the difficulties associated with carrying and caring for a child born as the result of violence.

Survivors of rape and their children are likely to be ostracized by their community. Married women may be "disowned" by their husbands. Unmarried women may never be able to marry because their communities consider them "spoiled". Raped women who are not able to marry or who have been abandoned are deprived of the "protection" and economic support that men are traditionally expected to provide in Sudan.[44]

Rape of women as punishment for their perceived political affiliation was also witnessed in Peru, where in the 1980s and 1990s security forces targeted for sexual abuse women whom they suspected of supporting the opposition armed group, Shining Path (Sendero Luminoso).[45] Hundreds of women were detained under the 1992 Anti-terrorism Law which suspended safeguards for people held in detention. According to Peruvian human rights organizations, most women detained under this law between 1992 and 2001 reported having been threatened with or subjected to sexual abuse; many of them were raped.

In the context of the continuing conflict in Chechnya, Amnesty International has received reports of rape and other sexual abuse of Chechen women by Russian soldiers. At the end of April 2004, Madina (not her real name) was detained by Russian federal forces on suspicion of being a Chechen suicide bomber. Madina, a 23-year-old with one child, was blindfolded and taken to the Russian military base in Khankala, where she was kept incommunicado for two weeks and allegedly tortured repeatedly. She said that electric wires were connected to her bra straps, and she was subjected to electric shocks. According to Madina, she was held in a wagon and she could hear the screams of other men and women who were also apparently tortured and held in different wagons within the military base.

Madina told Amnesty International:

"At some point there were eight of them in camouflage uniforms. And straight away swearing, no explanation. They stretched me on the bed. My hands were swollen. I was asking 'Where am I?' but they would shut my mouth ... they said: 'You are B-V-P'. [In Russian: "Bez vesti propavshyi" – 'disappeared'] *'You don't exist and time for you has stopped.'*

"They warned me on the first day that I would be begging to be dead. But at that time (in the beginning) I really wanted to live because I have my baby... I could not imagine that I would ask them for death... But on that day... exhausted, tired, breathless I started to ask them to shoot me."

Women who try to pursue complaints when they have been raped by members of the security forces risk further abuse. Twenty-year-old Gulsham Bano and her mother Raja Begum were gang raped by members of the Indian security forces in 1999, in the Indian state of Jammu and Kashmir. Rapes of women by all sides in the conflict have been reported there, particularly by the Indian Army. Since filing a complaint, both women and their entire families have been harassed by police and members of the army, and warned that unless they withdrew their complaint male members of their family would be killed by the security forces.

In some countries there are no procedures to safely report such abuse, as in Afghanistan. Amnesty International received reports that there was a riot by

The parents of 18-year-old Kheda Kungaeva hold up photographs of their daughter who was abducted and killed by a Russian army colonel in Chechnya in March 2000. There was evidence that she had been raped before her death.

women in an official detention centre in Herat in 2003 in response to sexual abuse by staff and that women held in Mazar-e-Sharif were assaulted by staff and members of armed factions in 2003.

Recent reports about torture or ill-treatment of Iraqi detainees by members of the Coalition Forces in Iraq have included allegations that women have been subjected to cruel, inhuman and degrading treatment. Sexual abuse, possibly including rape, has been reported and a military investigation headed by US Major General Antonio Taguba recorded various abuses, including a male guard having sex with a female detainee.[46] Some women detainees have spoken after their release to Amnesty International delegates under condition of anonymity. Their accounts included being threatened with rape, beatings, humiliating treatment and long periods of solitary confinement.

Hidden crimes

Rape and other forms of sexual violence often remain hidden for years or even decades. During the conflict in Guatemala in the 1980s, indigenous women associated military action with rape to such an extent that few volunteered information about it when investigators spoke to them about their experiences. International teams investigated the widespread human rights violations committed in the conflict at a time when the international community did not yet widely understand rape and sexual abuse as a form of torture. They were not trained to ask the relevant questions and as a result the massive scale of rape that took place has never been fully documented.

Conversely, in Bangladesh in 1971, the systematic rape of Bangladeshi women during the struggle for secession from Pakistan was reported widely. It is estimated that around one million people died and 200,000 women were raped.[47] After independence, the government of Bangladesh took a number of measures to deal with the aftermath of mass rape. Rehabilitation shelters were set up, international agencies arranged abortions and adoptions, and women rape victims were given a special title, *Bironginis* (heroines), in an attempt to reduce stigma. However, those who committed rape were not held to account. The main perpetrators, members of the Pakistani army, were held initially as prisoners of war and then returned to Pakistan. A number of their Bangladeshi collaborators were briefly arrested and subsequently released under a partial amnesty. Human rights groups focussed mainly on those imprisoned after the 1971 war, and years later, in the 1990s, researchers investigating the period found that while mass rape was widely acknowledged, there was no direct evidence available.

The long gap between the event and public discussion of it has become familiar to those who work on violence against women. The so-called "comfort women", women from at least 10 countries forced to work as sex slaves by the Japanese Imperial Army during World War II, also took decades to tell their stories.

Although today the investigation of sexualized violence in conflicts is more timely and thorough than in previous decades, this has not led to any corresponding increase in resources allocated to supporting the survivors.

Impact of rape and sexual assault

The impact and trauma of rape extend far beyond the attack itself. Women survivors face emotional torment, psychological damage, physical injuries, disease, social ostracism and many other consequences that can devastate their lives. After

the conflict ended in Rwanda in 1994, for example, 80 per cent of rape survivors were found to be "severely traumatized".[48]

Throughout the world, not only in countries in conflict, being publicly identified as a rape victim can so severely damage a survivor's status within her community that she will be reluctant to relate what has happened, even to those closest to her, for fear of ridicule, humiliation, rejection or ostracism. In Guatemala, some survivors are living in denial of what has happened to them. Although they suffer the psychological effects of their abuse, they attribute these only to a vague "sadness" (*tristeza*) rather than acknowledge even to themselves the brutality they have witnessed or endured.

The largest ever demonstration in Kaihin Park on the southern Japanese island of Okinawa sees tens of thousands of people protest against the rape of a girl by US servicemen, October 1995. Three US marines had abducted and raped a 12-year-old girl in Okinawa in September of that year. The US commander of Pacific Forces, Admiral Richard Macke, was forced to resign in November 1995 after suggesting that the three servicemen should have paid for a prostitute instead of raping the girl. It is a common misconception that allowing soldiers access to prostitutes helps protect the civilian population from sexual violence.

The attitudes they fear are not just held by men but permeate society as a whole. Several Burundian women who had been raped told Amnesty International delegates visiting the country in September 2003 that they had been mocked, humiliated and rejected by women relatives, classmates, friends and neighbours because of the abuse they had suffered. In Rwanda, rape survivors told Amnesty International delegates in 2004 that they had not only been humiliated and tormented by other women in their communities, but also by their own daughters.

In some parts of the world, women and girls who have been raped are shunned by their neighbours because of the fear that they have been infected with HIV. This, combined with attitudes towards rape, may lead to survivors being considered unmarriageable, with devastating consequences in societies where women's economic welfare and social standing is dependent on their relationship with men.

Cherifa Bouteiba, a married Algerian woman aged around 20, told Amnesty International that she had been living in constant fear since she was raped in 2001. She was abducted by seven armed men on 2 June 2001 while she was visiting relatives in Chlef province. She said she was taken to the mountains and repeatedly raped for two days before she escaped. She was pregnant at the time of the assault, and subsequently suffered a miscarriage. Her husband divorced her after the incident on the grounds that she had "soiled" his honour. She then became homeless as relatives were reluctant to house her for long, fearing her presence would put them in danger from armed groups. The authorities gave her no financial support. When interviewed by police, she was able to identify some of her attackers from photographs. Despite this, it appears that there was no further investigation of the crime.

The physical consequences of sexual assault include the effects of injuries sustained during the attack, pregnancies and sexually transmitted infections. Rape is often accompanied by extreme brutality. Women and girls are beaten; they have objects forced into their vaginas; and their genitals are mutilated. When sexual organs are torn or damaged during the assault, women may later suffer fistulas – the perforation of the wall between the vagina and anus – leading to incontinence and other serious conditions.

Rape survivors often have to finance their own healthcare. If they become pregnant, they face the option of either paying for an abortion (which is illegal in some countries) or bearing the cost of raising the child, even though the conflict may have displaced them or left them destitute. In many countries where rape has been used as a weapon of war, such as Burundi, Rwanda, Central African Republic and the DRC, there is no free state medical care.

Sexual slavery and sexual assault, including rape, constitute violations of women's right to health, among other rights.[49] In conformity with the right to health, women should have access to health services, including sexual and reproductive health services, which should meet standards of availability, accessibility, acceptability and quality.[50] Denial of such services to rape survivors severely compounds the human rights violations they have suffered. Under international human rights law, victims of human rights violations such as rape are entitled to a remedy, which must include medical care, both physical and psycho-social.

In societies where women and girls have suffered systematic rape, the risk of a rapid spread of HIV increases dramatically. There is also evidence that the violent nature of sexual attacks makes women and girls more susceptible to HIV and other sexually transmitted infections such as syphilis.[51] In Liberia, where an estimated 60 to 70 per cent of civilians suffered some form of sexual abuse during the conflict,[52] clinics in Monrovia reported in 2003 that all female patients tested positive for at least one sexually transmitted infection. Most of the patients said they had been raped by former government militia or armed opposition forces.[53]

It is not only the availability of medicines that influences the future of people with HIV/AIDS. Proper nutrition, psychological well-being, decent housing and personal and financial security are all factors that affect survival chances. In Rwanda, an

Ten years after the genocide of 1994, the women of Rwanda are still living with the consequences. Epiphane (not her real name) is 29 years old and has three children. *"My first husband was killed during the genocide. I had a three-month-old infant during the genocide, but was still raped by militia. I was in a Red Cross camp in the south of the country. The militia came every day to kill and rape... I learned I had HIV when I got tested before the birth of my youngest, in 1999. Since I learned I was infected, my husband said he couldn't live with me. He divorced me and left me with three children, so now I don't know how to pay for food, rent, school and so on. I have no family left. My six-year-old has many health problems, and she must have HIV. She should be on anti-retrovirals, but there isn't the money. Since I was married after the war, it is difficult for me to access help from the Genocide Survivors' Fund or other sources. My greatest worry is what will happen to my children if I die. I want to get sponsors for them, so at least I can die in peace."*

© AP Photo/Str

Women protest naked against the alleged rape, torture and murder of a local woman, Thangjam Manorama, by paramilitary soldiers in the north-eastern Indian state of Manipur, July 2004. Their demonstration outside the Assam Rifles base was one of many state-wide protests against the Armed Forces Special Powers Act, and led to the state government reducing the legal powers of military forces in a municipality in the area.

estimated 60 per cent of people with HIV/AIDS live below the poverty line. More than half of the population lacks access to clean water and 40 per cent are undernourished.[54]

Women refuse to be silenced

In some parts of the world, despite the stigma of rape, women have taken collective action against it. In India, for example, in the state of Manipur, some women's groups have mounted concerted protests against actions of the armed forces.

In mid-2004, soldiers of the Assam Rifles arrested a woman called Thangjam Manorama on suspicion of being involved in an armed group. She was formally arrested and forced to leave her parents' house with the army. The next day her mutilated body was discovered. Forensic evidence suggests that she was raped.

In protest at her death and the army's ability to rape and murder with impunity, a group of women expressed their disgust with the frequent atrocities committed by security forces against women and children. They stripped naked and publicly dared the soldiers to rape them. After this courageous and symbolic act, mass protests erupted all over the state leading to the state government asking the central government to withdraw the Armed Forces Special Powers Act. The state government declared that the Imphal municipal area was no longer to be categorized as a "disturbed area", so reducing the power of military forces in that location.

Chapter 4.
Devastated homes, ruptured lives

Rape is the most widely recognized form of violence against women in war, but there are many other ways in which women suffer particular forms of harm, or are affected disproportionately, when tension degenerates into armed conflict. Less attention has been given to the fact that women suffer disproportionately and differently from the economic, social and cultural aspects of militarization and war. However, the impact on women's right to food, water, housing, employment and education can pose as much of a threat to women's lives as physical forms of violence. Many women face gender-based abuses in situations of conflict, whether as refugees or internally displaced people, as civilians or as combatants.

Women and girls forced to flee from conflict

About 40 million people worldwide are displaced within their own countries or are refugees seeking protection abroad.[55] One of the major causes of such mass movements of people is armed conflict. According to estimates, 80 per cent of refugees are women and children.[56] In most areas of the world, agriculture or fishing are the main livelihoods of communities. Becoming a refugee often implies a complete break with livelihood cycles and a complete dependence on humanitarian agencies for basic survival.

Sometimes people are forced to flee not as an indirect result of conflict, but as an intentional strategy of war. This was the case, for example, during the conflicts in Central America in the late 1970s and early 1980s; in the former Yugoslavia in the 1990s; during the conflicts in the DRC, Liberia and Rwanda in recent years; and in the violence in western Sudan in 2004.

Women in flight are often the main providers of food, shelter and care for children – including children who are unaccompanied or have become separated from their families – and other relatives. Many are coping with the absence of male relatives who have been killed in the conflict, are involved in the fighting or have become separated from their families. The anguish of abandoning their homes for an uncertain and often hazardous journey is intense. The trauma of those who become separated from their children or parents in the chaos and confusion of conflict and flight can last a lifetime.

A refugee child from Sudan with seeds picked from nearby trees to hold off hunger, April 2004. The seeds would normally be cattle fodder. More than one million people have been forced to flee their homes in Darfur, western Sudan, where human rights violations are being carried out on a massive scale by the *Janjawid*, a government-backed militia, which often operates alongside government troops. By July 2004 at least 30,000 people were estimated to have been killed, and thousands of women and girls raped, often in front of family members.

Refugees and displaced people on the move face journeys involving physical hardship and lack of shelter, food and other basic necessities. The conflict in the DRC has resulted in approximately 2.7 million people, the majority women and children, being internally displaced after they fled their homes to escape from the various armies and militias. Aid workers have frequently been prevented from reaching them, leaving many without any support at all.

Women fleeing without the protection of their communities or male relatives face heightened risk of sexual violence, including rape. They may be forced to offer sex in return for safe passage, food, shelter, refugee status or documentation. In Colombia, the Ministry for Social Protection reported in 2003 that 36 per cent of displaced women in the country had been forced to have sexual relations with men.[57]

The loss of traditional support networks continues to have a negative effect on refugee and internally displaced women even after they have reached the relative safety of another area or country.

Women and girls who seek refuge in cities are often at grave risk of gender-based abuse including trafficking, exploitation and sexual violence. Many live in extreme poverty, magnifying the risk of abuse. Some destitute Afghan families who sought refuge in cities in Pakistan forced young girls into early marriages because they were unable to care for them or hoped they would be safer if married.

Fleeing women and girls who reach camps for internally displaced people or refugees may find that even in internationally supported camps, material assistance is minimal. In many areas, the level of international assistance in camps has fallen, in part as a result of decreases in funding.

What supplies there are may not be equitably distributed. Women and girls face discrimination in camps in the distribution of everything from food to soap and plastic sheeting. Refugee registration documents and ration cards are sometimes issued only to men, in their role as the head of the family. If these men abandon their families, their wives and children may be left unable to obtain any assistance.[58] In such circumstances, women and girls are extremely vulnerable to sexual exploitation, as the only means of accessing essential supplies for themselves and their families.[59] At the same time, some research points out that women who come to the camps as the head of their family feel they have gained new rights to make decisions about their lives and the lives of the children. They become important actors in the camps negotiating their rights and entitlements.[60]

Where families flee together, the strains of camp life can also lead to increased domestic violence and marital rape, as men vent their frustrations on women.[61] All the married women interviewed in refugee camps in Burundi by Human Rights Watch in 1999 reported experiencing domestic violence while in the camps.[62]

The physical layout of the camp can pose dangers if it has not been developed with women's needs in mind. Poorly planned camps can expose women to violence, including sexual abuse, from fellow refugees and camp officials. The need to ensure adequate lighting, readily accessible cooking fuel and safe housing is frequently ignored. In Uganda, for example, it was reported in 2002 that women were forced to leave the camp in search of water and firewood.[63] Some of them were abducted and sexually assaulted.

Sometimes, it is the very officials entrusted with their care, including peacekeepers and aid workers, who abuse displaced women and girls. Sexual violence and exploitation by peacekeepers and aid workers in camps in Guinea, Liberia and Sierra Leone has been reported, involving 40 different agencies. Interviews by UNIFEM with refugees in camps in these countries found that girls, the majority aged between 13 and 18, had been forced to exchange sex for cooking oil, wheat, medicine, transport, loans, educational courses and skills training.[64] The teenage pregnancy rate in the camps was estimated at 50 per cent.[65]

In May 2004, the UN launched an investigation into reports that its peacekeepers in Bunia, northeastern DRC, had sexually abused civilians, including women and girls. UN Secretary-General Kofi Annan has announced a UN policy of "zero tolerance" for such abuses and said that he is determined that the UN should enforce his Special measures for protection from sexual exploitation and sexual abuse, which he issued in a special bulletin in October 2003.[66] However, it remains unclear whether and how the alleged perpetrators of these acts will face justice or their victims receive redress.

According to a joint study by UNHCR and Save the Children-UK on sexual violence and exploitation of refugee children in Guinea, Liberia and Sierra Leone, peacekeepers are among the highest paying customers for sex with children. Some peacekeepers allegedly pooled money to obtain a girl and then all had sex with the same child.[67]

Other "clients" for girls forced to prostitute themselves in camps include refugee men who pay with money earned from trading, or by working for non-governmental organizations (NGOs) and international aid agencies.[68]

Supplies sometimes fail to address the specific needs of women, particularly access to contraception or reproductive healthcare. It is only recently, for example, that sanitary protection has been included in the UNHCR's list of essential supplies, even though the majority of refugees are women.[69] Without access to sanitary materials, women and girls are forced to remain at home and single women may even go without food if the regular food distribution takes place when they are menstruating.

Many refugee and displaced women do not have access to women doctors or health professionals. In Ethiopia and Zambia, for example, an independent assessment team was told that women and girls would not seek medical help because there were no women medical staff in the camps.[70]

Many of these problems stem from the fact that it is men, whether as officials or as refugee leaders, that plan, run and make decisions about resource allocations in refugee camps. They are often not sensitive to women's experiences and needs in conflict and as refugees. Cultural conditioning and taboos among the refugee population can also inhibit the participation of women in planning camps and decision-making.

Economic and social impact

Before and during conflict, gender stereotyping is usually reinforced and there may be increased control over women's freedom of movement or activities outside the home. In Israel and the Occupied Territories, for example, as conflict has intensified in the past decade, Palestinian and Israeli Arab girls have been more likely than their brothers to be withdrawn from school and women have been discouraged from going out to work.[71] Restrictions on the movement of Palestinians by the Israeli authorities have made it impossible for many Palestinian women to pursue their normal professions or reunite their families.

As conflict is signalled or initiated, heightened coercion to provide "traditional" female support services is common. Women are encouraged to be loyal and long-suffering wives, to enter the labour force to replace the men away fighting, to provide traditional "female" caring tasks – as cooks, carers and launderers – or to work as prostitutes. Such roles, often unpaid or badly paid, are sometimes coerced.

The allocation of gender roles means that the impact of conflict, and the death and destruction it entails, affects women and men differently. Losing family members causes immense emotional, social and economic suffering for all those left behind. Women have additional problems because of the disadvantage and discrimination they face in everyday life.

In Rwanda, for example, after the 1994 genocide, laws in areas such as inheritance discriminated against women. For example, women could not inherit property unless they were explicitly named as beneficiaries. Thousands of widows and daughters were left with no legal claim to the homes, land or bank accounts of their dead husbands or fathers. Widows whose husbands worked for state enterprises or large companies also faced great difficulties in obtaining their husbands' pensions. Women who had lost everything – families,

houses, property – found themselves raising their surviving children and the children of other dead family and friends with virtually no resources. Since 1994, the legislation on land rights has gradually been improved, but customary law, which often overrides written law, remains biased against women on issues of inheritance and land ownership.

Similarly, the emotional suffering of losing loved ones to "disappearance", without knowing what has happened to them, is sometimes compounded for women by the legal implications of not being able to prove their partner's death. In Guatemala, this meant that widows of the "disappeared" were unable to obtain state benefits.[72] In Algeria, the Personal Status Code has made it difficult for women to claim land or inheritance if their husbands or fathers have "disappeared". The report of an official commission of inquiry into "disappearances" in Sri Lanka, where tens of thousands of people

A family that fled fighting in Colombia shares a mattress in Lago Agrio, Ecuador, in a temporary shelter for Colombian refugees close to the border, July 1999. Hundreds of people left the Putumayo area as the security forces, army-backed paramilitaries and guerrilla groups battled for control of the region. Some three million people – the majority women and children – have been forced to flee their homes in Colombia in the past two decades amid escalating violence between parties to the conflict.

"disappeared" in the conflict in the late 1980s, recorded several instances where women were deprived of their lawful inheritance by their in-laws on the pretext that their husband was not necessarily dead.[73]

Sometimes, "disappearances" or killings have taken place on such a scale that communities have neither the resources nor customary practices to enable them to provide for widows and reincorporate them into the community.[74] Marriage and remarriage can be virtually impossible for women when there have been mass casualties of men during a conflict.

The resources and services that are damaged or destroyed by conflict often relate directly to women's traditional roles and responsibilities. Where women are responsible for providing food and water, for example, and the distribution systems have been polluted or destroyed, it is they who will have to wander further afield, often into minefields or areas where they may be at risk of sexual or other attacks, in search of supplies.

For example, four girls and a boy were killed by government soldiers in Laos as they foraged for food near the camp where they lived, in the Xaisomboune military zone, on 19 May 2004. The unarmed children, aged between 13 and 16 years old and part of an ethnic Hmong rebel group, were mutilated – the girls apparently raped before being killed – by a group of approximately 30 to 40 soldiers. The Hmong ethnic minority group in Laos has a long history of resistance to government control, and sporadic hostilities have continued for many years. Over the last two years, there has been an apparent increase in Lao government military activity against such rebel groups.[75]

Women are frequently expected to take on additional care responsibilities, such as looking after orphaned children or wounded relatives, despite the scarcity of resources. If homes have been destroyed, women may feel the loss most keenly, given that the home is in many cultures considered their traditional sphere. Women also suffer disproportionately from the practice of forced eviction. They often face subsequent discrimination in relation to property rights (including home ownership) and are vulnerable to violence and sexual abuse when rendered homeless.

In some circumstances, women find that they are no longer able to utilize their traditional skills and activities, such as food production, due to the destruction and pollution of conflict, or their own displacement. They may then be forced into illegal activities which can result in harassment, arrest or detention by the authorities. Women in Sudan, for example, who have fled north to escape the decades-long conflict in the south between government forces and the Sudan People's Liberation Army, have turned to illegal brewing. Many have been imprisoned, usually for four months, resulting in further hardship for their children.

Unwanted pregnancies, sexually transmitted infections and abortions often increase during and after conflict.[76] Women who choose to get pregnant can face health risks resulting from the breakdown in health and social services. Lack of medical care, combined with the physical and psychological pressures of conflict, leads to an increased incidence of miscarriage, premature labour, low birthweight babies and menstrual problems.

Generally, little healthcare is available for women and girl combatants in armed groups. This is particularly dangerous when female combatants give birth, often without any assistance for themselves or their babies. A doctor working at a hospital in Sierra Leone reported that babies of female combatants were so sick and malnourished that between 20 and 50 per cent of those brought to the hospital were dying.[77]

Women and girl soldiers

Women and girls carry out combat and support roles in armies and armed groups all over the world. Many are forcibly recruited and compelled to perform support tasks or act as sex slaves for their abductors. Some of them are young girls.

Worldwide, women make up less than three per cent of regular army personnel, although some armed forces have in recent years recruited more women.[78] The reasons for the growing recruitment of women in some countries include calls for greater gender equality, changes in the nature of the services required by the military, and demands for an increase in the size of the armed forces. Often, women serving in the military experience sexual harassment and violence. For example, a study found that at least 92 rapes were reported between 2001 and 2003 among the 43,000 troops stationed at US Air Force bases in the Pacific.[79]

Women soldiers who refuse the sexual advances of male colleagues may be accused of being lesbians and investigated for homosexual conduct, prohibited in many of the world's armed forces. The gender stereotyping that forms such an important part of the military ethos means that lesbians often find themselves subjected to homophobia, sexual harassment and dismissal because of their sexual orientation.

As in the regular military, female members of armed groups are most often given domestic support or menial tasks – carrying supplies and ammunition or messages, cooking, cleaning, laundering and sewing. Sometimes, they serve as spies, scouts, nurses or agricultural labourers. Because they are generally considered more expendable than men, they may be assigned dangerous roles and used as human shields, preceding their male colleagues into battle, or clearing minefields.

Democratic Republic of Congo

'It would be better if I died with the baby in my womb'

Rape and other war crimes, crimes against humanity and other grave human rights violations have been suffered on a daily basis by the civilian population of eastern DRC, who have seen combatants from around 20 armed factions fighting for control of the land and its resources.

Thousands of Congolese women of all ages, including young girls and elderly women, have been the victims of rape, abduction or sexual slavery. Many victims have been threatened with death, and punched, kicked, beaten with sticks and rifle butts or whipped. Some women have had a rifle, a knife, a sharpened piece of wood, glass or rusty nails, stones, sand or peppers inserted into their vaginas. Others have been shot during or after rape, sometimes in their genitals.

It is estimated that fewer than 30 per cent of Congolese have access to even basic healthcare. Because of the destruction of the healthcare infrastructure in the east, most women suffering injuries or illnesses caused by the rape – some of them life-threatening – are unable to access appropriate medical treatment.

The physical injuries that many of them have sustained require long and complex treatment. Many survivors of rape suffer: infection with HIV and other sexually transmitted diseases; uterine prolapses (the descent of the uterus into the vagina or beyond); fistulas and other injuries to the reproductive system or rectum, often accompanied by internal and external bleeding or discharge; urinary or faecal incontinence; a broken pelvis; infertility; psychological trauma and difficulties in maintaining normal sexual relations; difficult pregnancies and births; and prolonged menstrual periods accompanied by severe pains.

Only two hospitals in eastern DRC, run or heavily supported by international humanitarian non-governmental organizations, currently have the capacity and ability to provide surgery for rape survivors. They are only able to treat a small proportion of those in need. Many women cannot even reach these hospitals. Abortions are legal only in cases where the health of the woman is severely threatened, not in cases of rape.

The widespread fear of HIV/AIDS in eastern DRC contributes to the stigmatization of rape survivors and their children, as well as of others suspected of carrying the illness.

In April 2003, Sanguina and her friend Miriam were raped at gunpoint by three soldiers from one of the warring parties as they walked to their fields near Walungu, in South-Kivu. In October 2003, Sanguina was raped again, this time in her home, by another soldier. She became pregnant after this rape and in March 2004, when she told her story to Amnesty International, she was close to despair. "*In the community, they made such fun of me that I had to leave the village and live in the forest. Today, the only thing that I can think about is that I want an abortion. I am hungry, I have no clothes and no soap. I don't have any money to pay for medical care. It would be better if I died with the baby in my womb.*"

The DRC's healthcare infrastructure, always severely under-resourced, has broken down completely in many areas with the advent of war. It has been destroyed or looted by combatants or has become obsolete or neglected, with unhygienic conditions and no water or electricity supply. It also lacks human, material, logistical and financial resources. Professional psychological care is almost non-existent throughout the east. Outside the larger towns, access to emergency healthcare is available only to a handful of victims. Those who test positive for HIV rarely receive adequate counselling and only a tiny fraction of them receive treatment.

The DRC transitional government has displayed indifference to the issue of sexual violence and mass rape in eastern DRC and, beyond some isolated public condemnations, has shown no sign that it intends to take action to prevent sexual violence or to prioritize care and redress for survivors. Nor are the authorities taking meaningful measures to address the related issue of a burgeoning HIV/AIDS crisis in the country.

While the government and international community have put considerable effort and funds into planning the DRC's national elections, the delivery of basic healthcare in the east still relies almost entirely on overburdened local, national and international non-governmental organizations which lack the funding and capacity to meet the needs of the whole population.

Women combatants are also subjected to sexual abuse and exploitation. Amnesty International delegates in Colombia spoke to women who had been forcibly recruited into armed groups. Others had been enticed to join and then forced to cook, wash, mend, carry arms and serve as sex slaves. If they became pregnant, they were forced to have abortions. Pregnant women who did not want an abortion have sometimes run away from their units, but risked being killed if captured by their former comrades.[80] According to the Special Rapporteur on violence against women, many former combatants have spoken about being raped or sexually harassed by their male superiors as a first step in initiation.[81]

Child soldiers

Girls are an estimated 30 per cent of child soldiers. Child soldiers – under the age of 18 – are found in the military, armed groups, militia or paramilitary forces in 178 countries, according to a 2001 study by the Coalition to Stop the Use of Child Soldiers. Amnesty International actively opposes the voluntary or compulsory recruitment of both boys and girls under the age of 18.

Some girls become child soldiers to escape living in poverty, others to get away from physical or sexual abuse at home. Others are simply seized, a phenomenon which is most widely reported from Africa. Other recruits are motivated by political beliefs, revenge or a desire for respect.

Africa is the region with the highest number of child soldiers – approximately 120,000 children are believed to be in armed forces or armed groups.[82] In 2000, the Coalition to Stop the Use of Child Soldiers reported that in Peru, the Shining Path (Sendero Luminoso) armed opposition group had one of the largest contingents of girl combatants in the world, while in the conflicts in El Salvador and Uganda, approximately 20 per cent of child soldiers in armed groups were girls. There are a significant number of girl soldiers in the Maoist armed opposition in Nepal and in the Liberation Tigers of Tamil Eelam in Sri Lanka.

Many girl soldiers have been forced or coerced to serve as sex slaves – sometimes to everyone in the unit, sometimes as the "wives" of particular men. A Ugandan girl soldier reported: *"The rebel commander ordered the soldiers to come and choose among the girls to become their 'wives'. We were all lined up, and a man… came to me and raped me over and over again. I had to remain with… [him] every night for the two months I was in captivity."*[83]

In Angola, which has alternated between years of conflict and uneasy peace since it began its struggle for independence from Portugal in 1961, girls were expected to live with and sexually serve the chief and other men in their armed group. They were also forced to dance, entertain and sexually excite the men in preparation for battle.[84] If the girls refused any of these "duties," they were tied to trees and beaten with sticks or killed.

Women and girls are not recruited or forced into armed groups solely to serve as sex slaves. They also participate in combat, a phenomenon facilitated by the increasing prevalence of portable, affordable and easy to use weapons. Because of their size and agility, children may be sent on particularly hazardous assignments. Sometimes, as has been reported in Liberia and Sierra Leone, children are given drugs and alcohol to desensitize them to violence or inhibit fear.[85]

War, weapons and women

Modern warfare is characterized by the use of methods of warfare that result in civilians being killed and injured on a massive scale. In many conflicts civilians are deliberately targeted or fall victim because no effort is made to distinguish between combatants and civilians. Women, children and the elderly generally constitute the majority of the civilian population vulnerable to attacks, and are therefore in many instances disproportionately affected by such attacks.

Modern warfare also involves the use of weapons which do not distinguish between military and civilian targets, such as cluster bombs, which leave unexploded bomblets scattered over a wide area, and anti-personnel landmines. In Iraq in 2003 US forces reportedly used more than 10,500 cluster munitions containing at least 1.8 million bomblets. An average failure rate of 5 per cent would mean that about 90,000 unexploded munitions are now on Iraqi soil.[86]

Examining just one widely used weapon – the landmine – shows how a weapon which might appear to be gender-blind has effects and consequences which are in fact gender-specific.

Away from the battlefield, women are often exposed to more danger from landmines because of the kind of work they do, for example collecting water or firewood, growing food or taking produce to market. The majority of people fleeing conflict are women and children, and they often have to pass through combat zones and borders which are likely to be heavily mined. If they are injured by a landmine, women and girls are less likely to be treated and have less access to rehabilitation and artificial limbs. Injured men generally have priority access to scarce resources. Care responsibilities, or restrictions on women travelling unaccompanied, often make it difficult or impossible for women to seek treatment.[87] It may be considered unacceptable for women to be treated by male doctors.[88] Women and girls injured by mines are often rejected by their husbands, or find that they are unable to marry because of the social stigma attached to their disabilities.

Ahlam Abd al-Zahra Idris lost her legs after being wounded when her house in Basra, Iraq, was shelled by Coalition Forces on 21 March 2003. Her baby was wounded along with other members of her family. Twenty-three homes were hit on the same day and an estimated 31 civilians were killed.

Further dangers to women are created by the large number of arms often left in circulation after conflicts, together with habits of using force to solve problems. Violent disputes in the home often become more dangerous to women and girls when men have guns. There are thought to be around 639 million small arms in the world, produced by more than 1,000 companies in at least 98 countries. Eight million new weapons are produced every year.[89] They proliferate partly because government controls on the domestic and foreign transfer of such arms are riddled with loopholes.

Just under 75 per cent of all reported human rights abuses in Colombia between 1991 and 2001 were carried out with small arms or light weapons. In many countries the military firearm has become a status symbol and indicator of manhood and male virility. At the Acholi coming-of-age ceremony in Uganda, for instance, when a boy receives his first assault rifle he becomes a man: ashes are rubbed on his body, and everyone blesses the gun. In Somalia, parents have named baby boys "Uzi" or "AK".[90]

In Rwanda, medical professionals, local leaders and social workers who report a dramatic rise in rape in the years since the 1994 conflict consider that the availability of small arms in the region increases the capacity of perpetrators to commit acts of sexual violence and other crimes.[91]

At the other extreme, women are also affected in specific ways by chemical and radiological weapons. These pose a terrible risk to all of humanity, but they cause particular damage to women's reproductive health, and, potentially, genetic damage affecting future generations.

The use of chemical weapons by Iraqi forces against the Kurds of Halabja in 1988 killed an estimated 5,000 people outright and injured thousands more. By 1998 there were reports of growing numbers of children dying of leukaemia and lymphoma. In early 2004, an in-depth medical study suggested increased rates of infertility; babies born with disabilities; and skin, head, neck, respiratory, gastrointestinal, breast and childhood cancers among women and children present during the attacks.

Chapter 5.
Ending impunity

Rape and other gender-based violence during armed conflict have long been prohibited, both domestically and internationally, but these crimes are often ignored and rarely prosecuted. The reasons overlap with those behind the widespread impunity in peacetime for domestic violence and sexual abuse against women.

Perhaps even more than in times of peace, survivors of criminal acts of violence against women during armed conflicts have many difficulties in seeking justice. As a result, the perpetrators generally commit their crimes with impunity – they escape without being punished. Some of these difficulties are common to prosecutions for crimes against women in any context, particularly sexual crimes: women will not bring complaints or testify because they are afraid of being stigmatized, or fear further attacks; medical evidence is difficult or expensive to obtain; the authorities responsible for bringing prosecutions are indifferent; and the criminal justice system is biased against women. These problems are exacerbated in armed conflict where danger, confusion and lack of social order are common.

In recent years, the assumption that justice is an unrealistic goal in situations of conflict has been challenged, thanks to the activism of women's human rights defenders. They have publicized the experiences of women and used legal analysis to develop methods to hold individual perpetrators accountable. Through their advocacy, international criminal courts have been empowered to prosecute crimes of violence against women using more gender-sensitive definitions of crimes. Individual perpetrators of crimes of violence against women have been prosecuted. Some of the legal and practical difficulties common to prosecuting sexual crimes against women committed in peace and war have been addressed.

However, these impressive developments at the international level have had little effect in the vast majority of cases of violence against women in conflict. Impunity is still the norm. The international criminal system can only deal with a small number of cases. Therefore, states involved in armed conflict need to make a comprehensive effort to investigate cases, support victims and witnesses and bring the cases to trial fairly. More work needs to be done to ensure that women victims receive full reparation – rehabilitation, including healthcare; the opportunity to tell their stories in a dignified environment; compensation; restitution of lost homes, livelihood and property; guarantees that the crimes committed against them will not be repeated; and forms of satisfaction such as restoration of their dignity and reputation and a public acknowledgment of the harm they have suffered.

Barriers to justice

Securing justice for women during and after armed conflict through national legal systems has been and remains extremely difficult.

Many countries have discriminatory laws that make it difficult for women to access justice; conflict and its aftermath exacerbate the problems. Often women face difficulties because the laws in their country are inadequate to deal with sexual violence in conflict, or because laws are interpreted in ways that facilitate impunity. For example, national courts may have no jurisdiction over soldiers who are foreign nationals or it may be impossible to seek their extradition. The code of military law may not expressly address violence against women: the crimes committed may not be crimes under national law. Even where a military code does include crimes of violence against women, military investigations and prosecutions may not allow civilians the legal standing to bring complaints. Military investigation processes are often not independent and some allow military personnel to commit crimes with impunity.

In Mexico, for example, where a number of indigenous women have been raped by government soldiers in the state of Guerrero over the past decade, all the cases have been transferred to military jurisdiction, which has consistently failed to conduct proper investigations, guaranteeing that the alleged rapists go unpunished.

The administration of justice, including investigation, arrest of suspects, prosecution and functioning courts, is frequently destroyed or disabled by the armed conflict, so that pursuing complaints is difficult. Evidence, particularly medical evidence, can be hard to obtain in the disruption caused by conflict.

Sometimes problems in national criminal justice systems arise from indifference and discrimination against women. The general bias in criminal procedures and in the way evidence is taken makes it more difficult for women to access justice. Police, investigators and prosecutors frequently fail to take action on crimes committed against women, particularly where definitions of sexual crimes are dependent on notions of consent. Women who have suffered sexual violence under duress are seen to have agreed to sexual contact, when in fact they were simply too afraid to protest or refuse. As in peacetime, women are ashamed that sexual crimes were committed against them, fear stigma and rejection, are traumatized by the experience, and are afraid of further victimization. Without official support to ask for investigations, and protection from further crimes, they do not have the confidence to bring complaints and testify.

In some countries, the authorities do not wish to bring certain individuals to justice. Even after peace processes, perpetrators in armed forces may still maintain a powerful political position and use threats to maintain their impunity. The authorities may justify their reluctance to act in terms of keeping the peace, developing peace processes, or reintegrating former combatants. In the majority of cases, peace agreements are signed with little or no participation by women. National amnesty laws have been passed, and peace agreements signed, which grant immunity from prosecution for crimes including acts of violence against women. Such amnesty laws have been introduced in countries including Argentina, Chile, El Salvador, Peru and Sierra Leone.

However, after years of concerted work by human rights activists and others, at least in some of these countries progress is being made to have amnesty laws overturned. At the regional level, the Inter-American Court of Human Rights (and previously the Inter-American Commission on Human Rights) has stated that amnesty laws contravene the American Convention on Human Rights and international human rights law, and that the state has a duty to bring those responsible for human rights violations to justice.[92] In Peru, since the Inter-American Court ruling in 2001, prosecutors have opened investigations into cases of alleged human rights violations previously covered by amnesty laws. In Argentina, the Full Stop (*Punto Final*) law and the Due Obedience (*Obediencia Debida*) law gave immunity from prosecution for crimes committed during the "dirty war" of 1976 to 1983. These crimes included rape and other forms of torture. In August 2003, the Argentinian Senate declared these laws null and void. The Argentinian Supreme Court referred the issue of the constitutionality of the laws to the Appeal Court.

Colombia

'They would not accept my complaint'

"My daughter is nine years old. The events happened two years ago. I was at home with her and they were talking about rape on TV. My daughter lowered her head. 'Caliche touches me, he touches my vagina'. I was furious and I confronted Caliche. I told him I would bring an action against him. I went to the Attorney General's Office but they would not accept my complaint because they said that if it wasn't rape, they couldn't… He is from the AUC [Colombia's largest paramilitary group] in Combo del Hoyo, he's 19. He said that if I did anything to him, he would kill us." This testimony was given to Amnesty International on 15 November 2003. Nothing further happened as regards the complaint.

In Colombia, as elsewhere, sexual violence is rarely reported by the victim. When survivors muster the strength to complain, the authorities often seek to dissuade them. Even if they persist, the case is unlikely to be fully and independently investigated. The prospect of a conviction is virtually zero, especially if the alleged perpetrator is a member of the security forces, the army-backed paramilitaries or a guerrilla group.

A woman who seeks to bring a criminal action for offences involving sexual violence is expected to lodge a complaint, ratify it and then respond to summonses from the authorities to provide further information. If she fails to do so, the investigation may be closed. Human rights defenders have reported that some victims of sexual violence have been isolated from any legal or emotional support and subjected to abusive and humiliating questioning.

The Special Rapporteur on violence against women urged Colombia's Attorney General to appoint a high-level legal advisor to deal with sexual and gender-based violence. But such an appointment is yet to be made. Although Law 599 of 2000 makes it a punishable offence to inflict sexual violence on individuals who are protected under international humanitarian law, no investigations were known to have been carried out by the Attorney General's Office in line with such provisions by the end of 2003.

In January 2003, in an effort to pave the way for the "peace negotiations" with paramilitaries belonging to the AUC, the government issued Decree 128 which grants pardons to members of illegal armed groups who surrender to the authorities, provided they are not under investigation or in prison for human rights abuses. However, most members of armed groups responsible for human rights abuses, including sexual violence, have not been identified, so this decree may grant amnesties to those responsible for crimes of violence against women.

In Sierra Leone, the 1999 peace agreement between the government and the armed opposition provided an amnesty for combatants on both sides who had raped, maimed and killed civilians. The warring parties absolved themselves and each other. Within a year, atrocities were being committed again, rebel forces attacked UN peacekeepers and the peace agreement broke down. The international community was forced to reconsider the peace agreement and its amnesty, and took steps to set up an independent special court to try abuses committed in the conflict. However, abuses before November 1996 were excluded from the jurisdiction of the Special Court for Sierra Leone, and the amnesty continues to bar prosecutions for crimes not investigated or prosecuted by the Special Court.

Holding members of armed groups to account

Many of the acts of violence against women committed in conflicts around the world are committed by combatants who are members of armed groups. Holding them to account poses particular problems. Armed groups have a variety of different aims, and it is sometimes difficult to separate criminal from political objectives, whatever the group's professed aim. Some groups have a centralized command and control structure and operate within a clearly defined territory, others are loosely connected in transnational networks, with the capacity to strike almost anywhere in the world. Some armed groups have the explicit or tacit support or approval of the state, for example as paramilitary forces, and it is important that states not be allowed to shirk their responsibility to bring such forces under control.

There are many different – and passionate – views on whether and when it is legitimate to use force to achieve change or to confront state power. Amnesty International takes no position on this issue – it does insist, however, that groups which resort to force respect the rules of international humanitarian law and basic principles of humanity.

Common Article 3 of the Geneva Conventions applies in all cases of armed conflict, whether international or not, and to all parties to the conflict, as it reflects customary international law (law which is binding on all states, whether or not they are bound by treaty law). More detailed rules for non-international armed conflicts are included in Additional Protocol II to the Geneva Conventions. As a matter of customary law, basic human rights norms (directed for the most part towards states) apply to armed groups where they exercise *de facto* control over territory and take on responsibilities analogous to a government. Indeed, in a number of situations armed groups have expressly indicated their commitment to human rights principles. In any case, individual members of an armed group can and should be held criminally responsible for war crimes, crimes against humanity, genocide or other serious human rights violations.

Armed groups, no less than governments, must never target civilians, take hostages, or inflict torture or cruel, inhuman or degrading treatment, and they must ensure respect for basic human rights and freedoms in territory they control. Although international legal rules extend to armed groups, in practice these rules have had little impact, in part because of the difficulty of enforcing them and the lack of will to respect them.

In recent years armed groups operating in all regions of the world have been responsible for appalling human rights abuses, including brutal and systematic acts of violence against women.

Armed groups tend to operate either in opposition to state power, or in situations where state power is weak or absent. In either case, in practice it is difficult for the state in the territory affected to address – in a fair and effective way – the human rights abuses these groups commit. While this poses particular challenges, it does not mean that armed groups are beyond accountability. They remain accountable both in practice and legally.

On a practical level, they need and depend on support, resources and finance from other states, private organizations and sympathetic communities abroad and all of these can wield considerable control over armed groups.

On a legal level, the international tribunals for the former Yugoslavia and Rwanda have successfully prosecuted leading members of armed groups. The establishment of the International Criminal Court opens a number of new avenues for pursuing international criminal prosecutions, although it will only be able to investigate and prosecute a limited number of cases itself. Human rights advocates all over the world are seeking ways to pressure and engage armed groups to respect human rights, and these efforts must be strengthened. It is vital that investigations of human rights abuses begin as soon as possible, even before the conflict ends.

As part of the effort to persuade armed groups to respect human rights, greater attention must be given to ensuring that armed groups respect women's basic rights, and discipline forces under their command responsible for violence against women, in a manner consistent with human rights principles. This in itself poses challenges, as the methods of command and control within armed groups, and between armed groups and those exercising political control or moral influence over them, may be subtle, complex and opaque.

As membership of armed groups is frequently very informal and fluid, former members of armed groups often continue their lives without reference to their previous actions or roles, and with little fear of being brought to justice. In post-conflict situations, demobilization of armed groups is frequently a political priority, in order to achieve a political settlement. In particular, there is often pressure to act quickly to give former combatants work, pay and a position in society. However, without proper screening of former combatants and investigation of complaints of abuses, there is a strong risk that impunity persists. Perpetrators of atrocities may maintain positions of power and influence, including access to weapons and a licence to use force, particularly if integrated into post-conflict law enforcement bodies.

The informality of armed groups' membership sometimes enables perpetrators to flee abroad and seek protection in other countries as refugees. Article 1(F) of the 1951 Convention relating to the Status of Refugees denies refugee status when there are serious reasons for considering that the person has committed crimes against peace, war crimes, or crimes against humanity; serious non-political crimes outside the country in which they are seeking refuge or "acts contrary to the purposes and principles of the United Nations". Acts of violence against women by members of armed groups would be covered by this list. However, while this serves to deny perpetrators refugee status, international law requires them not to be returned to their country of origin if they would face torture, ill-treatment or other serious human rights violations there.

In cases where their return to their country of origin would put such perpetrators at risk, or where that country is unwilling or unable to bring them to justice, Amnesty International calls on all states to bring such perpetrators to justice in fair trials without the death penalty in the country in which they seek refuge, through the use of universal jurisdiction.[93] States should establish laws and methods of investigation to facilitate this. The use of universal jurisdiction is an important part of cooperation between states to bring perpetrators to justice, in cases where the state in which crimes took place are unwilling or unable to do so.

Using the international system

Some women have sought justice at the international level, where states have been unwilling or unable to bring perpetrators to justice.

International law has not always responded to crimes of violence against women in a way that addressed their needs. Since the 1990s, however, this has begun to change, as women's rights advocates and human rights organizations began to take action, using a variety of international arenas to transform the understanding of violence against women as a human rights issue.

© Paolo Pellegrin / Magnum Photos

The issue of violence against women in conflict rose in importance on the international agenda, particularly at the UN and in its human rights bodies. A vital step was taken in 1992 when the Committee on the Elimination of Discrimination against Women defined violence against women as a form of discrimination.[94]
Women's rights advocates participated in the Vienna Conference on Human Rights (1993), which confirmed that "women's rights are human rights".

In 2004, 10 years after the genocide in Rwanda, Suleman Muriandabigwi, a prisoner in Rimila prison, is brought before a traditional tribunal in Nyamata region to disclose where he buried his victims.

As a direct result of this effort, the UN General Assembly adopted a Declaration on the Elimination of Violence against Women[95] and the UN Commission on Human Rights appointed a Special Rapporteur on violence against women, its causes and consequences. Radhika Coomaraswamy, the first Special Rapporteur, spent nine years preparing reports on various aspects of violence against women, including in armed conflict, and carried out numerous fact-finding missions to countries where conflict had taken place. Her work, together with that of her successor, Yakin Ertürk, has resulted in a body of recommendations to individual governments and to the international community on the prevention of violence against women in conflict, as well as evaluating the progress made over a decade and the challenges ahead.[96]

The Fourth UN World Conference on Women, in Beijing (1995), outlined a detailed programme of action to ensure the prevention of violence against women. It called on states to take concrete action to investigate crimes and punish the perpetrators, and compensate and rehabilitate the survivors. The Platform for Action contains a detailed section on "Women and Armed Conflict". This lists wide-ranging measures recommended to achieve a number of strategic objectives including the following: "Increase the participation of women in conflict resolution at decision-making levels and protect women living in situations of armed conflict and other conflicts or under foreign occupation"; "Reduce excessive military expenditures and control the availability of armaments"; "Promote women's contribution to fostering a culture of peace"; and "Provide protection, assistance and training to refugee women, other displaced women in need of international protection and internally displaced women".

These influential declarations from UN conferences and the work of the UN treaty-monitoring bodies and Special Rapporteurs have developed the understanding of the obligations on states to take action to prevent and address violence against women. Alongside this process, women's rights advocates have worked to promote new ways of using international criminal law and international humanitarian law to secure convictions for crimes of violence against women. Their legal advocacy has ensured that individuals have been brought to justice for acts of violence against women, even when these were not at first investigated by the courts' prosecutors. Women's rights advocates helped to develop new definitions of crimes and rules of procedure to protect victims and witnesses through the international tribunals for former Yugoslavia and Rwanda. They used this valuable experience to campaign to establish an international criminal court which would bring justice for women one step closer.

Women's rights advocates faced many challenges, but over the years and decades, have gradually achieved a measure of success. International humanitarian law has traditionally prioritized the needs of those taking part in conflict, balancing considerations of humanity in warfare with "military necessity". Sexual violence against women has been understood as illegal in armed conflict for many centuries, but was previously couched in terms of "assaults against women's honour" which "presents women as male and family property" rather than as a crime against women's physical and mental integrity.[97]

The four 1949 Geneva Conventions, of which three focus primarily on the protection of combatants, explicitly prohibit rape, indecent assault and other crimes against women, as well as "any adverse distinction founded on… sex" in the treatment of "persons taking no active part in the hostilities". The adoption of two Additional Protocols to the Geneva Conventions in 1977 reflected an increasing recognition of the need to strengthen the protection of civilians in time of conflict. Differentiation in the level of protection on the basis of sex is only permissible when it favours women – women are accorded special protection in their capacity as mothers and prisoners with particular requirements.

As well as outlining rules for protection of civilians and others who are not taking part in hostilities (such as prisoners of war), international humanitarian law recognizes some acts as crimes. For example, the Geneva Conventions identify some crimes, such as torture and inhuman treatment, as "grave breaches" which require all states to seek out and prosecute perpetrators. Acts of violence against women, such as rape, were not expressly identified as "grave breaches".

In the 1990s, in response to the mass abuses of human rights which took place in former Yugoslavia and Rwanda, the international community examined crimes committed in conflict with renewed impetus. *Ad hoc* international criminal tribunals were established by the UN Security Council to look into crimes perpetrated during the conflicts in former Yugoslavia and Rwanda, and to bring to justice those responsible for war crimes, crimes against humanity and genocide.

The statutes establishing the *ad hoc* tribunals defined rape when part of an attack on a civilian population as a crime against humanity. However, they followed the Geneva Conventions and (in the case of the International Criminal Tribunal for Rwanda) Additional Protocol II, and consequently failed to define it expressly as a war crime. However, the tribunals did convict defendants of rape as a war crime – a violation of the laws and customs of war.

In the cases of *Akayesu*[98] and *Čelebići*,[99] rape was identified specifically as an act of torture when perpetrated by or at the instigation of a public official, and in the case of *Furundzija*, when it takes place during interrogation. In the case of *Kunarać* et al (known as *Foca*),[100] the defendants were convicted of rape as a crime against humanity and rape as a violation of the laws and customs of war (under Article 3 common to the Geneva Conventions). In the case of *Akayesu*, rape was identified, in the circumstances, as an act of genocide. The tribunals convicted men of acts such as sexual enslavement, forced nudity and sexual humiliation – in addition to rape and sexual assault – thus recognizing such acts as serious international crimes. The *ad hoc* tribunals addressed the impunity of members of armed forces and also of civilians. The tribunals confirmed that breaches of common Article 3 of the Geneva Conventions are war crimes. This means that members of armed groups, as well as members of official armies, can be held criminally responsible for their acts.

The rules of procedure and evidence of the tribunals, particularly of the International Criminal Tribunal for the former Yugoslavia, also made advances in addressing violence against women. While conscious of the need to protect defendants' rights, the sensitivities of victims and witnesses were a significant concern. To protect those willing to testify from the shame and stigma so often associated with rape, and from being targeted for new attacks by their assailants or others, the rules permitted the use of pseudonyms; allowed voices and photographic images to be electronically disguised; and agreed that transcripts could be edited to remove any reference to victims' identities.[101]

Other customary difficulties in sexual assault cases, which are also common to such cases in peacetime, were addressed. Sexual assaults and rape are often defined in terms of specific physical parts. For example, rape is defined in many jurisdictions as penetration of a vagina by a penis. The many different types of sexual attack, such as forced oral sex and insertion of objects into women's bodies, cannot be covered by such a restrictive definition. In the *Akayesu* case, the concept of "invasion" was developed, defining rape as "a physical invasion of a sexual nature".[102] This line of development was pursued so that the definition of rape as a crime against humanity in the Rome Statute of the International Criminal Court reflects it. Article 7(1)(g) (1) of the Elements of Crimes defines one element of the crime of rape thus: "*The perpetrator invaded the body of a person by conduct resulting in the penetration however slight, of any part of the body of the victim or of the perpetrator with a sexual organ, or of the anal or genital opening of the victim with any object or any other part of the body.*"

The *Akayesu* case defined rape as taking place in "circumstances which are coercive" and this line of reasoning has been used in many cases since. This is important, as international law recognizes that in situations of armed conflict, normal ideas of consent to sexual relationships cannot be seen as applying, given the circumstances of coercion and fear of violence.[103]

In many jurisdictions, it is difficult for a woman to persuade the court that she did not consent to sex, which usually leads to a finding that she was not raped and the acquittal of the perpetrator. In the tribunals, consent was not allowed as a defence if the victim had been subjected to, threatened with, or had reason to fear duress, detention or psychological oppression, or believed that if she did not submit, another person might be assaulted, threatened or put in fear.

The prior sexual conduct of the victim is frequently brought to the attention of courts to imply that she would be more likely to agree to sex and less likely to have been raped. The rules of procedure of the International Criminal Tribunal for the former Yugoslavia do not allow evidence of prior sexual conduct to be admitted as evidence.

The Tribunals were innovative and responsive to women's needs in recommending protective measures for victims and witnesses. They provided counselling and support for them, particularly in cases of rape and sexual assault. Support units for victims and witnesses were established by both tribunals, mandated to adopt a gender-sensitive approach and give due consideration to the appointment of qualified women gender specialists.

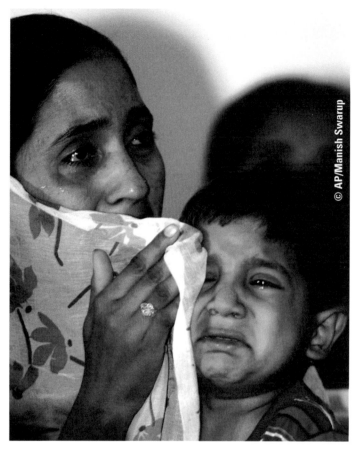

A woman holds her two-year old son as she testifies at a public hearing in New Delhi, India, April 2002. She saw one of her relatives raped and burned alive during inter-communal violence which took place in Gujarat in February 2002.

Slow but steady progress has been made in recognizing the enormity of sexual crimes, their devastating effects on survivors and the need to adopt a gender-sensitive approach in prosecuting and trying such cases. However, despite advances made by the tribunals, they have handled few cases and come to few verdicts. It is also telling that in the early cases, charges of sexual violence were not included in their original indictments, but were added later, after the submission of legal briefs by women activists. These were important experiences, as they assisted the gender-sensitive development of the International Criminal Court, particularly through the advocacy of the Women's Caucus for Gender Justice,[104] as well as other organizations, including Amnesty International.

The 1998 Rome Statute provided for the creation of a permanent International Criminal Court to prosecute people accused of genocide, crimes against humanity and war crimes. It confirmed developments in international law[105] in recognizing a broad spectrum of sexual and gender violence crimes as crimes against humanity and war crimes. These include rape; enforced prostitution, forced pregnancy and enforced sterilization; and gender-based persecution. Again, the inclusion of these crimes was due in large measure to lobbying by women activists and other organizations including Amnesty International.

The International Criminal Court Rules of Procedure and Evidence built on achievements of the tribunals regarding principles of evidence, *in camera* procedures, witness and victim protection, and gender sensitivity. The crime of sexual slavery received its first treaty recognition, and trafficking in people was recognized as a form of enslavement for the first time. The International Criminal Court was also empowered to award reparations. The need to ensure a "fair representation" of female and male judges was acknowledged,[106] as well as to appoint experts in sexual and gender violence as staff in the Registry and Office of the Prosecutor.

Major progress has been made in setting up the International Criminal Court since the entry into force of the Rome Statute on 1 July 2002. Ninety-seven states – almost half the international community – have ratified the Rome Statute, committing themselves to investigate and prosecute people accused of genocide, crimes against humanity and war crimes in their national courts.[107] The International Criminal Court will step in only when national courts are unable or unwilling to do so.

On 23 June 2004, following a referral by the government of the DRC, the International Criminal Court Prosecutor announced the opening of the court's first investigation into "serious crimes" committed in the DRC. This investigation will include crimes against humanity and war crimes such as murder, rape and torture that were committed after the International Criminal Court's jurisdiction began on 1 July 2002.

Challenges ahead

While these developments at the international level have established important principles and precedents, they have been extremely slow and costly, and have obtained relatively few convictions. Successful prosecutions at the international level are still largely limited to cases where rape and sexual abuse can be shown to be part of a pattern or strategy.

In addition, rape survivors run a heightened risk of ridicule, stigma and ostracism when they appear at high-profile international tribunals. Women who testify at such high-profile tribunals may also be in danger. A witness in the *Akayesu* trial heard by the International Criminal Tribunal for Rwanda, for example, was murdered along with her husband and seven children on her return from giving evidence. A witness in another case handled by the International Criminal Tribunal for Rwanda was also murdered. However, the Tribunal denies any link between the murders and its proceedings.

Sometimes the work of the tribunals is frustrated because the accused evades custody. For example, Charles Taylor, former President of Liberia, supported and encouraged the Revolutionary United Front, an armed opposition group responsible for gross human rights abuses against Sierra Leone's civilian population. He was indicted by the Special Court for Sierra Leone set up to establish responsibility for these atrocities. The terms of his indictment included: crimes against humanity, war crimes and other serious violations of international humanitarian law, including killings, amputations, sexual violence against women and children, forced labour including sexual slavery, and the use of child soldiers. However, he has so far avoided prosecution by leaving Liberia for Nigeria with implicit guarantees from the Nigerian government that he will neither be prosecuted in Nigeria nor handed over to the Special Court.[108]

Similarly, Indonesia has so far failed to cooperate with efforts by the General Prosecutor of the Democratic Republic of Timor-Leste (East Timor) to investigate and prosecute crimes against humanity and other serious crimes, including rape, carried out there by the Indonesian military and pro-Indonesian militia in 1999. To date, none of some 280 individuals living in Indonesia who have been indicted in Timor-Leste, including for rape, have been transferred to Timor-Leste for trial. None of the five cases investigated and brought to trial by Indonesia relating to the 1999 events involved rape or other crimes of sexual violence.

The International Criminal Court has been operational for only a short time, and has only recently begun its investigations. However, experiences at the international or mixed tribunals indicate that only a few cases each year will be brought for any crimes, and only in circumstances where national courts are unable or unwilling to prosecute. The Court has also faced political obstacles. The current US administration has consistently opposed the International Criminal Court since May 2002 when it launched a worldwide effort seeking to undermine the International Criminal Court and secure impunity for US nationals.[109]

International tribunals, in particular the International Criminal Court, are intended to act as a catalyst for the effective administration of justice at the national level. For all the gains at the international level, the struggle against impunity for violence against women in armed conflict will have to be fought primarily at the national level, where impunity for crimes of violence against women remains widespread.

Clearly, national systems must reform, so that like the international criminal law system, they become more gender-sensitive in their procedures, and re-examine their definitions of crimes to address the abuses that women experience in conflict. Gender-sensitive training should be given to all professionals involved in the criminal justice process, including the judiciary, police and prosecutors. When more courts address these cases effectively, as soon as possible after they were committed, there will be a much greater chance that perpetrators will be brought to justice. States must enact laws which allow them to cooperate in tracking down and arresting suspects, share evidence and either bring accused persons to justice in fair trials or extradite them to countries which are willing to try them.

Amnesty International is campaigning to ensure that the gender-sensitive developments in the International Criminal Court are incorporated into national legal systems. It calls on states to cooperate under the principle of universal jurisdiction. They should enact legislation so that those who commit genocide, war crimes and crimes against humanity – including and especially crimes against women – can be brought to justice in any court, even outside the country where the crimes took place. Amnesty International campaigns for prompt, effective, independent and impartial investigations to take place into abuses committed in armed conflict. Amnesty International lobbies with other non-governmental organizations to ensure that states emerging from conflict re-establish their judicial systems so that investigations can take place and perpetrators can be brought to justice in fair trials.[110] As with the International Criminal Court and the *ad hoc* international tribunals, punishments in national courts should exclude the death penalty.

Amnesty International also seeks to ensure that all states ratify the Convention on the Elimination of All Forms of Discrimination against Women, without reservations, and its Optional Protocol allowing individual petitions to the Committee on the Elimination of Discrimination against Women. It also calls on all states to incorporate international human rights standards into national law.

Pursuing reparations

Even if prosecutions are successful, many women survivors would not see this as the end of their struggle for justice. International human rights law requires reparations to victims and their families where abuses of human rights have taken place. This should include restitution (of, for example, lost homes,

livelihoods and property); compensation; rehabilitation; satisfaction (such as restoration of their dignity and reputation and a public acknowledgment of the harm they have suffered); and guarantees of non-repetition.

Family members grieve at a Mayan ceremony in Guatemala as the remains of victims of the armed conflict are exhumed, 1997. Women have played a vital role in the struggle for truth and justice after decades of conflict in Guatemala.

Currently provision of such reparations is extremely patchy, and usually non-existent. States should include provision of reparations in national legislation, and provide more assistance to women to allow them to rebuild their lives as fully as possible. Practical resources are necessary for this, and this is an area which has been overlooked in the past.

During the 1994 genocide in Rwanda, it is believed that some 250,000 to 500,000 women were raped; one third were reportedly gang-raped.[111] According to the Rwandan women's rights organization Haguruka, fewer than 100 rape cases have gone through the ordinary courts. Of the 20 or so defendants convicted, most were sentenced to death and have appealed against their sentences. Haguruka notes that women have little interest in bringing such cases because testifying, even behind closed doors, is traumatic and increases the chance that their communities will find out about the rape. There is an even more difficult struggle for justice for women who were raped by soldiers allied to the current government. It is virtually taboo to discuss crimes by government soldiers and only a few isolated cases have ever been brought to court.

Even survivors who take their cases to court are unlikely to receive any meaningful compensation. Suspected perpetrators are usually poor, especially if they have spent the past decade in detention without trial. A law to establish a compensation fund for victims has yet to be passed. The current government-funded Genocide Survivors Fund has been criticized by survivors as being inadequate and difficult to access.[112]

On a far lesser scale, but no less grave for the women themselves, victims of gender-based violence in the decades-long conflict in the Casamance region of Senegal continue to face a barrier of silence when demanding accountability from the Senegalese state. The impunity enjoyed for years by those responsible for human rights abuses in the Casamance conflict has deprived women of the right to truth, justice and financial compensation that would have enabled them to provide for their families by ensuring them a decent standard of living. An independent judiciary and the political will to deal with the past are key requirements if women are to have access to justice.[113]

While practical remedies such as compensation have received too little attention, the issue of truth commissions and truth-telling has become prominent in the international agenda. They offer the opportunity for women survivors to speak out about their experiences in a formal environment, to publicize what has happened to them and to have their experiences acknowledged. The non-judicial Tokyo Tribunal of 2000 fulfilled just this role for women survivors of forced sexual slavery by the Japanese army in World War II who had struggled for many years to secure an apology and compensation from the Japanese government. Women gave their testimonies and their experiences were acknowledged. The survivors were consulted fully on the process of the Tokyo Tribunal, and it was designed to address the need to have their experiences acknowledged.[114]

Women need to participate fully in the design and implementation of all truth and reconciliation processes in order to ensure that their voices are heard and their experiences considered in full.

The Peruvian Truth and Reconciliation Commission, which investigated human rights abuses by government forces and armed opposition groups during 20 years of internal armed conflict, is an example of how more recent truth commissions have made efforts to address patterns of violence against women which may remain hidden. More than 17,000 testimonies were gathered, and public hearings were held throughout the country, where more than 400 people testified, many for the first time. According to the Commission's 2003 report, although women were a minority among the victims, women suffered greatly during the conflict because of their gender, with rape being employed as a weapon of war to diminish them and keep them in their place through the use of their bodies. In the Commission's view, the internal conflict in Peru emphasized and strengthened a gender system that was characterized by inequality, hierarchy and discrimination. Women were ordered by both the armed opposition groups and the security forces to cook for them, tend the sick and provide accommodation while at the same time receiving threats from both. Women's views were not taken into account by either side, and the chronic racial, social and gender discrimination that exists in Peru contributed to the fact that the grief and suffering of thousands of women (and men) went unacknowledged for years.[115]

In certain conflict or post-conflict situations, non-judicial mechanisms may seem the only viable option for justice. For example, judicial institutions may have collapsed, or the number of suspects may make criminal prosecutions difficult, or it may be particularly hard to deal with certain abuses by armed groups. Such processes, however, should not preclude prosecutions or limit rights to reparations.

In Amnesty International's view, all supplementary or complementary mechanisms for justice must conform to international standards for fairness. They should be established in law, have a clear but flexible mandate that does not supplant the formal justice system, and provide adequate protection for victims, witnesses and their families. They should also be open and transparent, independent of the government and other political forces, have the necessary expertise, resources, investigative powers and time for their work, and have the power to make recommendations and award reparations.

Impunity for acts of violence against women is still the norm. Perpetrators are not investigated and brought to justice: women are not given the remedy they deserve. International standards, as developed in international human rights law and in the statutes and judgments of international tribunals and the International Criminal Court, should be fully reflected in all national jurisdictions. The norms that have been developed so far for addressing violence against women should be put into practice in investigations and prosecutions. More work needs to be done to develop methods of securing reparations for all victims, including those where perpetrators have not been brought to justice.

Chapter 6.
Women building peace

"Women are half of every community... Are they, therefore, not also half of every solution?"
Dr Theo-Ben Gurirab, Namibia's Minister of Foreign Affairs and UN Security Council President, speaking when UN Resolution 1325 was passed.

Conflict brings with it terrible human rights consequences for all involved – children, women and men. Conflict impacts on the civil, political, economic, social and cultural rights of women in particular ways, often with devastating effects. Increased violence against women, in particular sexual violence, appears to be endemic in conflict.

Attempts to address the human rights consequences of conflict, including the particular impacts on women, can only be comprehensive and long-lasting if women play an active part in all the relevant processes and mechanisms. To date, despite the undoubted efforts by international agencies to ensure that gender issues inform their work, the particular needs of women have all too often been neglected in disarmament, demobilization and reintegration programmes; repatriation and resettlement programmes; peace processes; peacekeeping initiatives; strategies to end impunity and prevent future conflict; and in reconstruction programmes. Yet women's participation in the planning and implementation of these processes is fundamental to ensuring that they address the human rights of all – including women.

UN Secretary-General Kofi Annan has acknowledged this. *"Efforts to resolve these conflicts and address their root causes will not succeed unless we empower all those who have suffered from them – including and especially women. And only if women play a full and equal part can we build the foundations for enduring peace – development, good governance, human rights and justice."*

Further, the UN Secretary-General has recognized the link between women's participation in efforts to resolve conflicts and their wider participation in society. *"If women do not participate in the decision-making structures of a society, they are unlikely to become involved in decisions about the conflict or the peace process that follows."*[116] Amnesty International believes that the international community – the UN and all governments – has an obligation to ensure women's full participation in peace processes and negotiations to reconstruct their country and their future.

UN Resolution 1325

In 2000, the fundamental principle of women's participation was recognized in UN Security Council Resolution 1325. The Resolution builds on a number of initiatives that reflect a growing awareness of the abuses suffered by women in conflict. These have included the appointment of a Special Rapporteur on violence against women, its causes and consequences, in 1994; the Fourth World Conference on Women, held in Beijing in 1995; the appointment of a Special Rapporteur on the question of systematic rape and sexual slavery and slavery-like practices during wartime, in 1995; and the Windhoek Declaration and the Namibia Plan of Action on Mainstreaming a Gender Perspective in Multidimensional Peace Support Operations, in 2000.

Resolution 1325 not only draws attention to the particular impact of conflict on women, it also recognizes "the consequent impact this has on durable peace and reconciliation". And, perhaps most importantly, it recognizes women as indispensable actors in finding solutions.

The resolution calls on all parties to armed conflict to respect international humanitarian law and to "take special measures to protect women and girls from gender-based violence, particularly rape". But the groundbreaking nature of Resolution 1325 lies in the repeated message throughout that the role of women should increase, at all decision-making levels, in the prevention, management, and resolution of conflict and in peace processes. It refers to women's involvement in UN field-based operations, and especially among military observers, civilian police, human rights and humanitarian personnel. It calls for the particular needs of women and girls to be considered in the design of refugee camps; in repatriation and resettlement; in mine-clearance; in post-conflict reconstruction; and in disarmament, demobilization and reintegration programmes. Women need to be involved from the start in all aspects of reconstruction.

In response to Resolution 1325, two highly significant documents were produced in 2002. UNIFEM (the United Nations Development Fund for Women) published *Women, War, Peace: The Independent Experts' Assessment on the Impact of Armed Conflict on Women and Women's Role in Peace-building*;[117] and the UN Secretary-General carried out a study, entitled *Women, Peace and Security*.[118] Both made valuable far-ranging recommendations. However, much needs to be done if the principles of Resolution 1325 are to become a reality. For example, UNIFEM, mandated to provide financial and technical assistance to promote women's human rights, political participation and economic security, remains the smallest UN fund.

Working for peace with justice

Resolution 1325 and other breakthroughs in acknowledging and combating the particular impacts of conflict on women have been the fruit of women's struggles at local, national and international level. These same women and groups have actively disseminated Resolution 1325 throughout the world, advocating its vigorous use to protect women and help reconstruct societies. They have campaigned to end the abuses of women's human rights that are so widespread in situations of conflict and militarization.

Many women's groups have joined across national, ethnic, political and religious divides to make their voices heard in peace processes and help end the conflicts that impact so negatively upon women's rights. Such coalitions have been seen in places as diverse as Papua New Guinea (Bougainville), United Kingdom (Northern Ireland), Israel/Occupied Territories, Serbia, Solomon Islands, Sri Lanka and the three countries of the Mano River Union: Guinea, Liberia and Sierra Leone.

In Israel, activists of Women in Black have for the past 16 years stood at road junctions, dressed in black, every Friday afternoon, for an hour, often facing threats and abuse, to protest against the continued occupation of Palestinian Territories. Other Israeli women, outraged by the Israeli Defense Force's treatment of Palestinians, came together as Machsom Watch (Checkpoint Watch) to monitor a particular roadblock. They hoped their mere presence and questioning might serve as a brake on the soldiers' behaviour and help them see the Palestinians as human beings. The group is now monitoring roadblocks all over the West Bank.

Some of these successful campaigns have been attained at a cost. Women human rights defenders and women working to end conflicts across the globe continue to be at grave risk.

An Indonesian woman protests in Jakarta on 23 May 2003 against the internal armed conflict in Nanggroe Aceh Darussalam (NAD) between Indonesian government forces and the armed independence group, the Free Aceh Movement (GAM). Following the declaration of a military emergency in NAD on 19 May 2003 there was a significant deterioration in the human rights situation in the province. Both the Indonesian security forces and GAM have committed serious human rights abuses. Violations allegedly committed by the security forces include rape and other forms of sexual violence against women.

In Colombia women who speak out for their rights face intimidation, violence and even death from armed groups on both sides of the country's long-running internal conflict. Rape, mutilation and violence against women and girls have been used by army-backed paramilitaries and the security forces to generate fear and to silence campaigns for social, economic and political rights. On 21 July 2003, "Angela" was kidnapped by alleged paramilitaries. She was a leading member of ANMUCIC, the National Association of Peasant, Black and Indigenous Women of Colombia, in the department of Cundinamarca. She was held captive for three days before being released. While in captivity, she was physically and psychologically tortured and subjected to serious sexual abuse. She had to flee the country a few months later. *"There was a grey truck with dark windows. They grabbed hold of me roughly and threw me inside. They had cartridge belts and were wearing military uniform. They asked me my name, trampled on me and started driving off. It must have been about six hours before they let me out. I asked where we were going and they said that they were taking me for a drive. They tied me up, it was dark and I was thirsty and very afraid. They hit me and insulted me and asked me about other ANMUCIC leaders, they…"* She was unable to continue her account as the memory of what she went through that day came back to her and she broke down, sobbing.[119]

Barriers to participation

Women have, for many years, been active in campaigning around conflict, human rights and peace. Despite the strength of this work, much of it has been carried out against the odds, often participating in informal processes. But the will of women to participate fully in formal processes too should not be doubted. Women's participation in formal peace processes has been known to bring issues to the table that might otherwise not have been included.

The wider pattern of discrimination that women face and the particular impact of conflict upon them often lie at the heart of women's lack of participation in both formal and informal processes. The briefest of surveys shows that the list of economic, social and cultural hurdles that women need to overcome is formidable.

Women's participation is hindered by the fact that they are more likely to have fled conflict. They are particularly likely to have shouldered economic and social responsibilities as primary carers and providers for dependants – both their own and, in some cases, those of their extended family or other members of their community. They often take on additional work as resources become increasingly scarce. The health of women and girls may be undermined as diets become more restricted and preference is given to other members of the family. All of these factors make participation in formal or political processes more difficult.

Women are more likely to be subjected to cultural pressures not to put themselves forward, to refrain from travel, and not to engage in important public arenas. Political groups that take forward formal processes are usually male-dominated. Women are less likely to have received an education or training or to have "relevant" working experience – things that are often perceived as necessary requisites to participation in formal processes. Their education is likely to have been disrupted by the conflict.

In some countries women face intimidation as a direct result of their participation. Afghan women delegates to the Emergency *Loya Jirga* (grand assembly) in June 2002, for example, which debated the post-conflict future of the country, were intimidated and threatened by members of armed groups loyal to powerful regional commanders.

Vulnerability to violence underpins many of the constraints on women's participation. In conflict and post-conflict situations, restrictions on women's movement and activities often increase. The lack of physical security for women – the breakdown of law and order – often results in women feeling unable to travel, or being prevented from travelling by male relatives seeking to protect them. In Iraq, for example, the security vacuum following the US-led invasion and occupation in 2003 saw daily newspaper reports of kidnappings and rape. Many women and girls gave up work and study and remained at home. Fear of sexual violence may lead to an increased incidence of early marriage, again often coinciding with increased constraints on activities and movements. For example, in early 2004, an increase in early marriage was noted among Sudanese girls in refugee camps in Chad.

Access to social networks can also affect women's participation in many processes. Social networks – especially those involving women – may have broken down in times of conflict. If they have not, some women may be excluded from them as a result of the ostracism that often stems from sexual violence. In some cases, conflict has actually resulted in more positive changes to women's status and in the creation of new social networks. However, such changes are often transitory and rapidly reversed when conflict ends. In addition, changes in gender roles at the local level have often not been accompanied by corresponding changes in political or organizational influence.

In some situations women fear that their participation might harm their reintegration into society and their marriage prospects. This is particularly the case with former female combatants who fear that society will assume – rightly or wrongly – that their role in the military was one of sexual slavery.

Women's organizations also cite lack of resources as one of the basic obstacles they need to overcome. Participation in peace processes and reconstruction efforts, political activism and campaigning, dissemination of information and reaching out to women throughout a country or region are all costly. When such activities are most crucial, resources are most scarce, and labour is often diverted elsewhere.

All these factors form barriers to women's participation in the planning and implementation of disarmament, demobilization and reintegration programmes, repatriation and resettlement programmes, peace processes and post-conflict reconstruction. Unless more creative thinking is applied in order to overcome such barriers, women will remain absent, their voices will not be heard, and issues of particular importance to women are likely to be ignored.

Demobilization and reintegration of combatants

In Mozambique, when the long civil war between the government and RENAMO finally ended, women and girls associated with combatants as "wives", cooks, agricultural labourers and porters often found themselves in one of two undesirable situations. Some were left by the side of the road as RENAMO soldiers boarded vans to return home under demobilization and reintegration programmes. Others found themselves having to accompany their captors – men who had raped and abused them – to cantonment sites (where former combatants are housed pending demobilization and reintegration).

In Sierra Leone, many girl and women combatants were not given the chance to communicate in private with UN personnel implementing demobilization and reintegration programmes. This left those who wished to leave the men who had abducted and sexually abused them unable even to express their wishes.

Although accurate data is not always available, in some countries there is a clear gap between the number of women and girls actively involved in conflict and the number demobilized. For example, a study undertaken by the non-governmental organization Save the Children showed that up to 5,000 girls were directly involved in conflict in Liberia between 1989 and 1997, yet few girls were demobilized. Following a peace agreement in 2003 to end the conflict which resumed in 1999, of 71,000 combatants disarmed and demobilized by 30 August 2004, 12,600 were women and 1,356 were girls.[120] In Sierra Leone, approximately 30 per cent of child soldiers in rebel forces were estimated to be girls. Yet between 1998 and 2002 only 8 per cent of the 6,900 children who were formally demobilized in the country were girls.

The absence of women and girls from disarmament, demobilization and reintegration programmes stems in part from a narrow understanding of who the beneficiaries of such programmes should be. In Sierra Leone, for example, many girls and women did not receive the benefits available as part of the demobilization and reintegration programme because they were regarded as non-combatants or dependants, even though they had been forcibly recruited to provide sexual and other services to the armed groups. In Mozambique so unquestioned was the assumption that those in need of demobilization and reintegration are men, that the demobilization package contained only men's clothing. Women and girls who have played different roles may be ignored, yet are also in need of reintegration into society.

Sometimes lack of participation in demobilization programmes has been connected to the eligibility requirements, including surrendering arms or ammunition. In some situations commanders have been known to take arms away from combatants, effectively preventing them from participating. Sometimes female combatants have had to hand over their arms to male combatants, and have then failed to qualify for assistance.

Although the most recent process in Liberia did not originally require women and children to hand in arms or ammunition, this requirement was introduced in some places. This apparently happened because of the larger than expected number of combatants coming forward, in order to exclude those not eligible for the benefits of the programme. At the demobilization site in Tubmanburg, Bomi County, UNMIL (UN Mission in Liberia) officials explained to Amnesty International representatives in July 2004 that children, and women, were now required to surrender a weapon or ammunition in order to qualify for assistance. This was also reported to be the case in Zwedru, Grand Gedeh County, where disarmament and demobilization began in early July 2004.

Women and girl soldiers trying to reintegrate into society have particular needs, some of which stem from the abuses they have suffered and the social and cultural attitudes confronting them.

Women combatants – whether forcibly recruited or not – and girls may have particular physical and mental health needs as a result of sexual violence and other abuses. They may need immediate access to ante-natal or post-natal care. They may need protection from those who abused them during the demobilization process, including in disarmament and demobilization sites (cantonment sites). Women and girl former combatants trying to reintegrate into society face particular attitudes regarding their expected role in the community. They may also be socially stigmatized because of their experiences, including the abuses they may have suffered. Some find themselves ostracized and isolated.

© AP/Charles Dharapak

Afghan refugee women attend a gathering to discuss peace and solidarity in Afghanistan in December 2001. More than 500 delegates attended the meeting in Peshawar, Pakistan, to talk about refugee repatriation and the role of women in ensuring human rights in Afghanistan.

Children – boys and girls alike – generally have particular educational needs as a result of having been deprived of schooling during their time as child soldiers. Education is key for their successful rehabilitation and reintegration and reduces the risk of their taking up arms again.

Former women combatants may have particular material needs arising from discriminatory laws regarding property ownership and – if they have been widowed – inheritance.

The experiences of former child soldiers – especially those who have lost their family – may vary according to their gender and the gender role they are expected to play.

Some demobilization and reintegration programmes have recognized the particular needs of women and girls and attempts are being made to learn from previous mistakes. In Liberia, for example, the plans for the disarmament,

Colombia

Gender-blind demobilization

In Colombia one particular demobilization campaign provides an example of the dangers of failing to integrate a gender perspective into such processes. The campaign in question not only failed to acknowledge women's needs, it actively helped to perpetuate and strengthen gender stereotypes.

In November 2002 a dispute ensued after it was revealed that leaflets containing pictures of scantily dressed women had been distributed by the army to "invite" combatants in armed groups to demobilize. Colonel Manuel Forero, director of the *Programa de Atención al Desmovilizado*, an army programme to assist demobilized combatants, revealed that 3-5 million copies had been printed and had been distributed in the special security zones, the Rehabilitation and Consolidation Zones (*Zonas de Rehabilitación y Consolidación*), set up by the government in the departments of Sucre, Bolívar and Arauca. The colonel told the media that "it is just an appetizer in the campaign to tell the guerrillas that they are welcome".

The army also distributed leaflets in Medellín with the picture of a woman dressed as a guerrilla and the phrase, "Young guerrilla, are you bored?" In response to the hostile reaction from women's organizations, the Defence Minister stopped the distribution of the leaflets. Colonel Forero had defended the leaflets by stating that "It's an aggressive campaign to sell a product". He added that he did not know why the designers had chosen to use the female figure.

demobilization, rehabilitation and reintegration process following the August 2003 peace agreement acknowledged the particular difficulties facing girls and women. Separate camps or areas within cantonment sites were to be provided. A network of women's organizations with expertise in counselling victims of sexual violence, reproductive health and psycho-social support would provide assistance and support. Access to healthcare, basic education, skills training and personal development counselling was to be provided to all demobilized girls.

The test for the programme will be to see how many women and girls are able to participate and to see whether longer-term rehabilitation and reintegration are achieved. The broader test is to ensure that this experience is used in other disarmament, demobilization and reintegration programmes. Failure to do so will have far-reaching consequences.

When programmes fail to recognize the needs of women and girls, they may drift back to the groups that abused them as their only option in order to survive – even if they were forcibly recruited and sexually abused in the ranks and had no desire to return. Other women may turn to prostitution in order to survive. Asked by Amnesty International if she would ever consider going back to the army, Jeanne, a young woman forcibly recruited by an armed group in the DRC in 1996 at the age of 11, responded: *"A year ago my answer to that question would have been no. But now I'm sorry to say, having been demobilized, that yes, I do miss the army... now, a year on from being demobilized, I've got nothing. They haven't found a way of reintegrating me into the community or enabling me to resume my studies, although we specifically told them that we wanted to study. There's nothing... We don't exist..."*

Repatriation and resettlement programmes

Repatriation and resettlement programmes are frequently planned and implemented with little or no participation from women, and little or no understanding of or provision for women's experiences during conflict and displacement. Their needs for successful and safe repatriation and resettlement are routinely overlooked.

Women who attempt to return home on their own face many potential dangers, whether from continued fighting, or because they have to pass through heavily mined areas. Once home, they may find themselves living alongside the very people who killed their relatives or raped them. Conflict may have destroyed their environment, making agriculture impossible. As single women, they may be unable to inherit land or property previously owned by dead or missing male relatives, leaving them unable to support themselves and their children.

In Rwanda, for example, discriminatory laws meant that thousands of women widowed in the genocide could not legally inherit the property of their late husbands or claim their pensions. One survivor interviewed by Human Rights Watch in 1996 said: "*Someone once told me that it is better to live through a war than after a war. I understand that now.*" Another said: "*Women lost their families, their houses, their property – everything. Now they have to raise their surviving children and the children of other dead family and friends... Many women who have lost everything have taken in other people's children. But they do not get the property that comes with these children which could help them live... They stay in abandoned houses, yet fear putting money into them and then losing it to the former owners. They are often chased from the family property.*"

Some women may never be able to return home, or may be displaced for many years or even several generations, as in Angola and the Occupied West Bank and Gaza Strip. Salim and 'Arabia Shawamreh, for example, are from Palestinian families who originally lost their homes when their village in the northern Negev was destroyed by Israeli forces at the time of the establishment of the State of Israel in 1948. Successive generations of their families lived in the overcrowded Shu'fat refugee camp in Jerusalem, until Salim and 'Arabia were finally able to buy a plot of land and build a house on it in 1993. The Israeli authorities, however, demolished this home, in 1998. Subsequent attempts to build new homes suffered the same fate in 2001 and 2003.

Refugee and displaced women and their children may be denied a range of social, cultural and economic rights. For example, in Colombia and the Balkans displaced women have reported that their children are not allowed to attend local schools.

Others may be forcibly deported to a conflict zone and threatened with sexual abuse if they resist. In April 2003, a 23-year-old Colombian woman was reportedly threatened by members of the Panamanian Guard seeking to deport her. They allegedly threatened to bury her alive, forced her to strip at knifepoint and threatened to rape and mutilate her. She was among more than 100 Colombians deported from Panama between 18 and 21 April 2003. The deportees, most of whom were Afro-descendants, were filmed or photographed while being forced to sign or put their fingerprint on documents stating that their deportation was voluntary.

Those who seek permanent asylum abroad can experience difficulties because gender-based persecution may not be recognized by the authorities as a justification for granting refugee status. Sometimes interviewers and interpreters are men and have little experience or understanding of the needs and experiences of women asylum-seekers. Women asylum-seekers may also be reluctant to tell male interviewers about the gender-based abuses they have suffered.

Women who are resettled in third countries have specific needs as women, because of the situations they fled, and often, because their customs and culture differ from those of their host country. These needs are frequently not understood and therefore overlooked. Resettlement efforts may also favour boys over girls. In November 2000, for example, a US programme brought 4,000 "lost boys" from Sudan to the USA to help them escape and overcome years of violence and deprivation. Not one girl was included in the programme, even though hundreds of girls were living in the Sudanese countryside with no homes or food, and there were many girls living in the same camps from which the boys had been chosen.

Reconstructing society, preventing future conflict

Crucial to any peace process is the planning and implementation of post-conflict reconstruction and mechanisms for the prevention of future conflict. Women's participation is key. Successful reconstruction that addresses the needs and respects the rights of all parties is, in fact, a crucial element of conflict prevention. Resolution 1325 calls on all participants to adopt a gender perspective. This should include, "Measures that ensure the protection of and respect for human rights of women and girls, particularly as they relate to the constitution, the electoral system, the police and the judiciary".

The experiences of women during conflict, including as victims of sexual violence, must be fully recognized in the post-conflict era. This means addressing impunity and providing reparations for abuses suffered. It also means that every structure and institution that is rebuilt must weave the necessary protections against repetition into their very fabric. Guarantees of non-repetition have long been recognized as a form of reparation. The post-conflict context provides a unique opportunity to provide these to society as a whole.

At the very heart of protection against repetition of human rights abuses against women, including rape and sexual violence, is the principle of non-discrimination. The Special Rapporteur on violence against women noted with regard to Afghanistan, in her 2004 report, that, "The drafting of a new constitution provides a valuable opportunity to guarantee the principle of equality of rights for women and men and to prohibit all forms of discrimination against women." In order for peace to respect the rights of all, such non-discrimination needs to reach into every corner, including issues as far-ranging as post-conflict justice; policing; the legal system, including especially the legal framework concerning violence against women, and land, property, inheritance and family law; education; health and economic policies.

Amnesty International has made detailed recommendations, for many countries, on the ways in which protection of women's rights can be built into the institutions of society in periods of transition. Such recommendations have ranged from the recruitment of women police to training for the judiciary on

Democratic Republic of Congo

Government indifference

"There is a future before us that we are determined to live."
Rape survivor, DRC

The DRC has been wracked by war since August 1998 which is still having a devastating impact, despite a series of international and national peace agreements in late 2002 and early 2003 that brought an official end to hostilities.

If women in the DRC are to rebuild their lives, and have futures safe from violence, the abuses women and girls have suffered throughout the conflict must not be ignored. These women are entitled to see perpetrators brought to justice and to receive reparations. Discrimination at every level must be addressed, to allow them to move forward.

The legal system discriminates against women in many ways. For example, under the Family Code, a married woman who wishes to take a case to court must first ask her husband's permission. Moreover, in the Penal Code "rape" is not adequately defined.

Not only should discriminatory and inadequate laws be reformed, but the army and the police must receive gender-sensitive training on international human rights and humanitarian law and on handling cases of violence against women. The health system needs to be rebuilt, taking into account the needs of women. Steps must be taken to give girls and women the same opportunities for education as boys and men. Public awareness programmes should be put in place to combat the social and economic exclusion of rape survivors.

To date, the tens of thousands of women and girls living with the aftermath of rape and sexual violence have also had to cope with the indifference of the state and the international community. A UNAIDS[121] officer in Kinshasa told Amnesty International researchers in June 2004, *"We had thought that it was because their attention was focused on political questions in a situation that was so difficult that it was impossible to formulate an adequate response [to the plight of survivors of sexual violence]; but now we are in a period of pacification of the country, we would have thought it was time to talk about it and take action."*

handling cases of violence against women; from changes to laws on so-called "honour" crimes to the introduction of penalties for forced and early marriage; from the carrying out of detailed research and data collection on the incidence of violence against women to establishing programmes of education and outreach concerning women's human rights. Such recommendations are always tailored to the specific context and the specific needs of women in particular countries. The common themes throughout are the fundamental principles of non-discrimination and respect for and protection of women's human rights.[122]

Never again: listening for the signs

Effective early-warning systems can play a significant role in the prevention of future conflict and its attendant human rights abuses. Some argue that a gender perspective on early-warning systems increase their effectiveness by making them more alert to the impact on women.

The Commission of Experts appointed by the UN Secretary-General to investigate violations of international humanitarian law in the former Yugoslavia referred to at least 2,000 reported cases of sexual violence. It identified rape by individuals or small groups of men in conjunction with looting and intimidation as a pattern occurring before hostilities began in a particular area.[123]

A joint paper from the non-governmental organization International Alert and the research institute Swiss Peace Foundation states, "A gender-sensitive focus may enrich our understanding of factors that lead up to armed conflict…the process of engendering early warning…ensures that the concerns of men and women are equally considered, to benefit men as well as women." It identifies gender-sensitive indicators such as propaganda emphasizing aggressive masculinity; media scape-goating of women, accusing them of political or cultural betrayal; and engagement of women in shadow war economies.[124]

The independent experts' report, *Women, War and Peace*, notes the potential contribution of women to early-warning systems, but laments the lack of mechanisms to facilitate such contributions.

The UN study, *Women, Peace and Security*, points out that rising militarism and nationalism in the early stages of conflict can affect attitudes to women, reinforcing gendered roles and restricting their enjoyment of human rights. Increases in violence, including violence against women, and changes in gender roles are indicators that can be usefully integrated into early warning systems. The role of the media in reporting events is also significant, given the media's potential to inflame tensions.

Chapter 7.
Recommendations

Violence against women, as defined in international standards, is prohibited at all times, in all its forms, by international and regional treaties, as well as by customary international law.[125] Even in times of armed conflict, women and girls have the right to be free from crimes which constitute violence against women.[126] Situations of conflict, military occupation and militarization often lead to a greater incidence of violence against women, including but not limited to sexual violence, which require specific protective and punitive measures.[127] Women's experience of these forms of violence differs depending on a number of factors including race, class, ethnicity, sexual orientation, age, nationality and economic situation.

Amnesty International's campaign seeks to complement and contribute to the efforts of women's organizations and others to combat violence against women before during and after armed conflict. Amnesty International calls on all involved to implement measures for the prevention of violence against women. It also seeks to promote a broader human rights agenda, calling for women's full participation in processes relating to conflict prevention, conflict resolution and peace-building.

To effect real change, action is needed now, internationally, regionally and nationally. Amnesty International is urging that the following steps be taken as a matter of urgency and is calling on all governments, as well as individuals and organizations, to ensure that they are carried out.

All governments must respect, protect and fulfil women's right to freedom from crimes of violence, both in peacetime and in armed conflict. All other parties to armed conflict, and those in a position of influence, must similarly ensure that these and other fundamental rights are not abused.

To that end, the international community, governments and other parties to armed conflicts must act without delay.

1. **Condemn violence against women in any circumstances – all parties to armed conflict must:**

   - Publicly denounce gender-based violence, whenever and wherever it occurs.

   - Issue clear instructions to their forces to refrain from all forms of violence against women.

   - Train all their armed forces and other personnel on the rights of civilians and combatants no longer participating in hostilities to protection, including the prohibition of violence against women.

2. **Commit to ending impunity for violence against women – governments (and where appropriate armed groups) must:**

   - Ensure that laws, rules, regulations and military orders prohibit violence against women and provide for disciplinary and criminal punishments for perpetrators, while respecting human rights standards.

   - Establish adequately funded, independent and transparent monitoring and inquiry mechanisms with the power to promptly investigate any credible allegations of violence against women and make public their findings.

   - Suspend from duty, pending investigation, any member of the police, security forces or other state organization implicated in violence against women.

   - Bring all those responsible for acts of violence against women to justice in fair trials that pay attention to the particular needs of women subjected to violence, including sexual abuse, and exclude the death penalty.

   - Ensure that crimes of violence against women and other human rights violations committed by soldiers against civilians are not subject to military jurisdiction.

   - Cooperate in bringing to justice perpetrators of serious crimes by armed groups through the exercise of extraterritorial jurisdiction and support for international judicial bodies such as the International Criminal Court.

- Exclude crimes relating to sexual and other forms of violence against women from amnesty provisions.

- **Armed groups** should establish accountability within their ranks for any acts of violence against women, ensuring that any disciplinary measures are consistent with basic human rights and humanitarian principles.

3. **Provide full, effective and prompt reparations to survivors of violence – governments, the UN and other relevant international bodies must:**

- Facilitate national and international programmes of humanitarian assistance to survivors of violence, including providing emergency healthcare programmes.

- Ensure that all survivors of violence have access to reparations, including compensation, restitution, rehabilitation, satisfaction and guarantees of non-repetition.

- Ensure adequate provision of programmes that provide medical, psychological, social and legal support for survivors of rape and other forms of sexual violence, including those living with HIV/AIDS.

- Launch public awareness campaigns to challenge the stigma aimed at survivors of sexual violence and people living with HIV/AIDS.

4. **Take steps to prevent violence against women in armed conflict – all governments must:**

- Encourage and support monitoring mechanisms to combat violence against women, which should establish time-bound and measurable targets to end violence against women.

- Maintain reliable, up-to-date statistics on the incidence of and complaints relating to violence against women and how they are dealt with, in order to develop gender-sensitive policies, programmes and service delivery for women.

- Introduce education and public information programmes to help eliminate violence against women and to counter prejudices and gender stereotypes about men and women that can give rise to it. Custom, tradition, religion or culture should not be invoked to avoid governments' obligations to eliminate such violence. Governments should encourage the media to observe and promote respect for women's physical integrity and ensure that any incitement to gender-based violence is prohibited in law and practice.

- Ensure the increased representation of women at all decision-making levels in national, regional and international institutions and mechanisms for the prevention of conflict.

- Repeal or amend discriminatory laws which constitute or facilitate violence against women, or which act as a barrier to accessing remedies for violence, including in the areas of property rights and inheritance, and access to healthcare, housing, work, property, food and water.

5. **Ensure violence against women is prohibited in national law as a criminal offence with effective penalties and remedies for all forms of violence against women in armed conflict – all governments must:**

- Ratify, without reservations, and implement through national law relevant international human rights and international humanitarian law treaties (see Appendix). Implement fully other relevant standards including the UN Declaration on the Elimination of Violence against Women, UN Security Council Resolution 1325 on women, peace and security, and the Beijing Declaration and Platform for Action. Ratify the Convention on the Elimination of All Forms of Discrimination against Women, without reservations, and its Optional Protocol allowing the right of individual petition.

- Ratify the Rome Statute of the International Criminal Court and enact implementing legislation. Enact legislation permitting the exercise of universal jurisdiction for crimes under international law, including genocide; crimes against humanity; war crimes; torture including rape, sexual slavery, enforced prostitution, forced pregnancy, enforced sterilization, or any other form of sexual violence of comparable gravity; extrajudicial executions; and "disappearances".

6. **Ensure that peacekeeping and other field operations forces do not violate women's human rights – the UN and all governments contributing to these operations must:**

- Develop and enforce codes of conduct for all their forces to protect women from gender-based violence, including sexual exploitation and trafficking.

- Ensure that all such forces are adequately trained in the protection of women's human rights, for example by distributing the UN Secretary-General's Bulletin, *Special measures for protection from sexual exploitation and sexual abuse*, and ensuring that its provisions are effectively observed.

- Employ staff with the expertise and capacity to protect women from violence, including through monitoring and investigating allegations of abuse.

7. **End the misuse of arms to perpetrate violence against women – all governments must:**

    - Stop the manufacture, transfer, stockpiling and use of landmines and ratify, implement and monitor the 1997 Mine Ban Treaty.

    - Respect and enforce arms embargoes to prevent transfers that could contribute to grave human rights abuses and impose effective controls on all international and national arms transfers to ensure that they are not used to commit human rights abuses, including violence against women.

    - Effectively remove unlawful weapons at the community level by working with women's organizations and other civilian community organizations and ensure these organizations are effectively involved in peace agreements and disarmament, demobilization and reintegration programmes.

    - Support efforts to agree an international arms trade treaty to help stop the proliferation of weapons used to commit human rights abuses, including violence against women.

    - Impose and enforce a moratorium on the use of cluster weapons; and on the use of depleted uranium weapons pending authoritative conclusions on their long-term effects on health including women's health.

8. **End support and assistance for governments and armed groups which could result in violence against women – all those providing such support, whether other governments, businesses or organizations, must:**

    - Publicly condemn all forms of violence against women.

    - End the provision of any logistical, financial or military assistance to governments or armed groups which could reasonably be assumed to result in violence against women.

    - Use their influence to stop further abuses by governments or armed groups they have been supporting.

9. **Provide assistance and protection to refugees and internally displaced women – governments, the UN and other relevant international bodies must:**

    - Give effective protection to refugee and displaced women from sexual and other exploitation by all involved, including international humanitarian workers.

- Involve women in the design, planning and running of all camps for refugees or internally displaced people and in repatriation and resettlement programmes.

Schoolgirls taking part in the launch of AI Benin's Stop Violence Against Women campaign in Porto-Novo, Benin in 2004.

- Take into account the health and other needs of women and ensure that adequate resources are provided.

- Establish an effective, independent and transparent mechanism to investigate complaints of violence against women that occur in camps for refugees or internally displaced people.

- Ensure that agencies which provide protection for asylum-seekers, refugees and internally displaced people are adequately resourced.

- Ensure that asylum policies take into account persecution on the basis of gender, including the risk of sexual violence in armed conflict zones; and that all refugee and displaced women are registered individually and issued with their own separate identity documents.

10. Stop the use of child soldiers – all parties to armed conflict must:

- Make a public commitment not to recruit into their armed forces those under the age of 18 or to employ them directly in hostilities, and hold to that commitment.

- Set up programmes to demobilize, disarm and rehabilitate child soldiers that take into account the rights and particular needs of girls.

- Give priority to rehabilitation schools, improving access to basic education for girls and encouraging vocational training and higher education for girls and young women.

11. Ensure that human rights defenders can carry out their work without fear – all parties to armed conflict must:

- Publicly commit to ensuring that human rights defenders working on violence against women and other human rights issues can carry out human rights work in situations of armed conflict without fear of retaliation or punishment by adopting, publishing and implementing a comprehensive policy on the right to defend human rights which:

  ○ strengthens support for the role of human rights defenders and fully respects the provisions of the UN Declaration on Human Rights Defenders;

  ○ includes action to ensure that human rights defenders have unrestricted access to survivors of abuses, especially women, in areas affected by armed conflict;

  ○ includes action to recognize and protect the unique contribution of women human rights defenders to the promotion of human rights.

12. Involve women fully in peace processes – all governments, the UN and relevant international bodies must:

- Implement UN Security Council Resolution 1325 in full.

- Ensure that women play a key role in the design and implementation of all peace-building initiatives.

- Ensure that women have full access to the resources and services provided by post-conflict reconstruction initiatives.

- Incorporate a gender perspective and promote gender equality in all peace processes, agreements and transitional government structures, ensuring that women have the right to participate at all levels of decision-making.

- Pay special attention to the health, rehabilitation and training needs of women in disarmament, demobilization and reintegration initiatives.

Appendix: International standards

The following international and regional treaties and other standards should be ratified and implemented, or (as the case may be) taken into account by governments and other parties to conflict to stop violence against women in conflict-related situations:

Treaties

- International Labour Organisation (ILO) Forced Labour Convention (1930).
- UN Charter (1945).
- UN Convention on the Prevention and Punishment of the Crime of Genocide (1948).
- Geneva Conventions of 1949 and their Additional Protocols of 1977.
- European Convention on Human Rights and Fundamental Freedoms (1950).
- UN Convention relating to the Status of Refugees (1951) and its Protocol (1967).
- UN Convention relating to the Status of Stateless Persons (1954).
- ILO Abolition of Forced Labour Convention (1957).
- UN Convention on the Reduction of Statelessness (1961).
- International Covenant on Civil and Political Rights (ICCPR) (1966).
- International Covenant on Economic, Social and Cultural Rights (ICESCR) (1966).
- (African Union) Convention Governing the Specific Aspects of Refugee Problems in Africa (1969).
- American Convention on Human Rights (1969).
- UN Convention on the Elimination of All Forms of Discrimination against Women (CEDAW) (1979) and its Optional Protocol (2000).
- African Charter on Human and Peoples' Rights (1981).

- UN Convention against Torture and other Cruel, Inhuman or Degrading Treatment or Punishment (1984).

- Inter-American Convention to Prevent and Punish Torture (1985).

- European Convention for the Prevention of Torture and Inhuman or Degrading Treatment or Punishment (1987).

- Additional Protocol to the American Convention on Human Rights in the area of Economic, Social and Cultural Rights (1988).

- UN Convention on the Rights of the Child (CRC) (1989).

- African Charter on the Rights and Welfare of the Child (1990).

- UN Convention on the Protection of the Rights of All Migrant Workers and Members of Their Families (1990).

- Inter-American Convention on Forced Disappearance of Persons (1994).

- Inter-American Convention on the prevention, punishment and eradication of violence against women (1994).

- Convention on the Prohibition of the use, stockpiling, production and transfer of antipersonnel mines and on their destruction (1997).

- Rome Statute of the International Criminal Court (1998).

- Optional Protocol to the Convention on the Rights of the Child on the involvement of children in armed conflict (2000).

- UN Convention against Transnational Organized Crime (2000).

- UN Protocol to Prevent, Suppress and Punish Trafficking in Persons, especially Women and Children (Trafficking Protocol, also known as Palermo Protocol) (2001).

- Optional Protocol to the Convention on the Rights of the Child on the sale of children, child prostitution and child pornography (2002).

Declarations and other standards

- Universal Declaration of Human Rights (1948).

- UN Declaration on the Protection of Women and Children in Emergency and Armed Conflict (1974).

- UN Code of Conduct for Law Enforcement Officials (1979).

- UN Declaration of Basic Principles of Justice for Victims of Crime and Abuse of Power (1985).

- Committee on the Elimination of Discrimination against Women, General Recommendation 19, Violence against women (1992).

- UN Declaration on the Protection of All Persons from Enforced Disappearances (1992).

- UN Declaration on the Elimination of Violence against Women (1993).

- Vienna Declaration and Programme of Action (1993).

- The Cairo Declaration: Programme of Action of the International Conference on Population and Development (1994).

- Beijing Declaration and Platform for Action (1995).

- UN Guiding Principles on Internal Displacement (1998).

- UN Security Council resolutions on children and armed conflict, 1261 (1999), 1314 (2000), 1379 (2001).

- UN Declaration on the Right and Responsibility of Individuals, Groups and Organs of Society to Promote and Protect Universally Recognized Human Rights and Fundamental Freedoms (1999).

- UN Security Council Resolution 1325 (2000).

- Durban Declaration and Programme of Action (2001).

- UN High Commissioner for Human Rights, Recommended Principles and Guidelines on Human Rights and Human Trafficking, UN Doc. E/2002/68/Add.1 (2002).

- UN Secretary-General's Bulletin, Special measures for protection from sexual exploitation and sexual abuse, UN Doc. ST/SGB/2003/13 (2003).

Endnotes

1 *Sudan: Darfur – Rape as a weapon of war: sexual violence and its consequences* (AI Index: AFR 54/076/2004).

2 *Sudan: Systematic rape of women and girls* (AI Index: AFR 54/038/2004).

3 *Solomon Islands: Women confronting violence* (AI Index: ASA 43/001/2004).

4 UN Security Council Resolution 1325 (2000) on Women and peace and security.

5 UN Declaration on the Elimination of Violence against Women, Article 1.

6 Committee on the Elimination of Discrimination against Women, General Recommendation 19, Violence against women, (Eleventh session, 1992), UN Doc. HRI\GEN\1\Rev.1, para 6.

7 Fourth World Conference on Women, Beijing, September 1995, Action for Equality, Development and Peace, Beijing Declaration and Platform for Action, UN Doc. A/Conf.177/20 (1995), para 136.

8 Rehn, Elisabeth, and Sirleaf, Ellen J., *Women, War, Peace: The Independent Experts' Assessment of the Impact of Armed Conflict on Women and Women's Role in Peace-building*, UN Development Fund for Women (UNIFEM), 2002, p.17.

9 Report of the Special Rapporteur on violence against women, *Towards an effective implementation of international norms to end violence against women*, UN Doc. E/CN.4/2004/66, 26 December 2003.

10 Gardam, Judith G. and Jarvis, Michelle J., *Women, Armed Conflict and International Law*, Kluwer Law International, 2001, p.1.

11 *Report of the UN Secretary-General on the causes of conflict and the promotion of a durable peace and sustainable development in Africa*, UN Doc. A/52/871 - S/1998/318, para 4.

12 Report of the Expert of the Secretary-General, Graça Machel, *Impact of armed conflict on children*, UN Doc. A/51/306, para 24.

13 "Non-state actors" is a term often used to describe entities other than states, including private individuals, groups of inidividuals and organizations. Amnesty International believes that these non-state actors, including armed groups and economic actors such as businesses, have a responsibility to respect basic human rights and humanitarian principles.

14 "Anti-Terror Measures Delaying Green Cards", *Washington Post*, 23 September 2004, p. AO1.

15 These include: *It's in our hands – Stop Violence Against Women* (AI Index: ACT 77/001/2004); *Mexico: Intolerable Killings – 10 Years of abductions and murder of women in Ciudad Juárez and Chihuahua* (AI Index: AMR 41/026/2003); *Colombia: "Scarred bodies, hidden crimes" – Sexual violence against women in the armed conflict* (AI Index: AMR 23/040/2004); *Democratic Republic of Congo: Mass rape – Time for remedies* (AI Index: AFR 62/018/2004); *Solomon Islands: Women confronting violence* (AI Index: ASA 43/001/2004); and *Sudan: Darfur: Rape as a weapon of war – sexual violence and its consequence*, (AI Index: AFR 54/076/2004); *Kosovo (Serbia and Montenegro): "So does it mean that we have the rights?" – Protecting the human rights of women and girls trafficked for forced prostitution in Kosovo* (AI Index: EUR 70/010/2004).

16 The World Health Organization has described "collective violence" as the use of instrumental violence by people who identify themselves as members of a group, whether temporary or permanent, against another group or set of individuals in order to achieve political, economic or social objectives. This term can be applied not just to situations of armed conflict but to a broader range of situations of violence, the boundaries of which are frequently blurred. (see www.who.int/violence_injury_prevention/violence/collective/collective/en).

17 Additional Protocol II to the Geneva Conventions, Article 1 (2).

18 According to the Stockholm International Peace Research Institute, world military spending increased by 18 per cent in real terms between 2001 and 2003, to reach US$956 billion in 2003. See also, *Rights at risk: Amnesty International's concerns regarding security legislation and law enforcement measures* (AI Index: ACT 30/001/2002) and "Resisting abuses in the context of the 'war on terror'" in *Amnesty International Report 2004* (AI Index: POL 10/004/2004).

19 See for example, *Broken bodies, shattered minds: Torture and ill-treatment of women* (AI Index: ACT 40/001/2001); *Mexico: Intolerable Killings – 10 years of abductions and murder of women in Ciudad Juárez and Chihuahua* (AI Index: AMR 41/026/2003); and *Turkey: Women confronting family violence* (AI Index: EUR 44/013/2004). See also: www.amnesty.org/actforwomen.

20 *Report of the Special Rapporteur on Violence against Women to the World Conference against Racism, Racial Discrimination, Xenophobia and Related Intolerance*, 2001, UN Doc.A/Conf. 189/PC.3.

21 Sharp, Rhonda, *Gender-disaggregated Beneficiary Assessments: Gender budget initiatives within a framework of performance oriented budgeting*, UNIFEM, July 2003.

22 Petchesky, Rosalind P, *Global Prescriptions. Gendering Health and Human Rights*, Zed Books, 2003, p.123 and p.132.

23 See for example Chinkin, Christine: "A gendered perspective to the International Use of Force", *Australian Year Book of International Law*, 1988. See also Charlesworth, H. and Chinkin, C., *The Boundaries of International Law: A Feminist Analysis*, Manchester University Press, 2000.

24 *Threatened existence: A Feminist Analysis of the Genocide in Gujarat*, International Initiative for Justice in Gujarat, 2003, p.29.

25 Testimonies from Guatemala collected by Amnesty International in the late 1970s and early 1980s.

26 *Crimes of Hate, Conspiracy of Silence – Torture and ill-treatment based on sexual identity* (AI Index: ACT 40/016/2001).

27 *Colombia: "Scarred bodies, hidden crimes" – Sexual violence against women in the armed conflict* (AI Index: AMR 23/040/2004), p.39.

28 These same values have contributed to the belief of some military hierarchies that the exclusion of homosexuals, particularly gay men, enhances values critical to performance, such as unit cohesion, morale and discipline.

29 Charlesworth, H. and Chinkin, C., *The Boundaries of International Law: A Feminist Analysis*, Manchester University Press, 2000.

30 Goldstein, Joshua S., *War and Gender: How Gender Shapes the War System and Vice Versa*, Cambridge University Press, 2001.

31 Charlesworth, H. and Chinkin, C., *The Boundaries of International Law: A Feminist Analysis*, Manchester University Press, 2000; Moser, Caroline and Clark, Fiona (eds), *Victims, Perpetrators or Actors? Gender, Armed Conflict and Political Violence*, Zed Books, 2001.

32 Enloe, Cynthia, *Does Khaki Become You? The Militarization of Women's Lives*, Pluto Press, 1983, p.24.

33 Immunity is given by Regulation 2000/47 on the Status, Privileges and Immunities of KFOR and UNMIK and their Personnel in Kosovo, UNMIK (the interim UN mission in Kosovo), 18 August 2000.

34 *Kosovo (Serbia and Montenegro): "So does it mean that we have the rights?" – Protecting the human rights of women and girls trafficked for forced prostitution in Kosovo* (AI Index: EUR 70/010/2004), p.72.

35 *The Health Risks and Consequences of Trafficking in Women and Adolescents, Findings from a European Study,* London School of Hygiene & Tropical Medicine (LSHTM), 2003, p. 31.

36 González, Rebeca, *Violencia Intrafamiliar: Fruto de las armas de fuego,* Instituto de Enseñanza para el Desarrollo Sostenible, Guatemala, 1996.

37 Lindsey, Charlotte, *Women facing War,* ICRC, 2002, p.40. See also *Rwanda: "Marked for Death" – Rape Survivors Living with HIV/AIDS in Rwanda* (AI Index: AFR 47/007/2004), p. 2.

38 "Domestic violence against Palestinian women rises", *Middle East Times,* 20 September 2002, based on reporting from *Agence France-Presse.*

39 *Israel and the Occupied Territories: Surviving under siege – The impact of movement restrictions on the right to work* (AI Index: MDE 15/001/2003).

40 Rehn, Elisabeth and Sirleaf, Ellen Johnson, *Women, War, Peace: The Independent Experts' Assessment of the Impact of Armed Conflict on Women and Women's Role in Peace-building,* UNIFEM, 2002, p. 17.

41 Enloe, Cynthia, *Does Khaki Become You? The Militarization of Women's Lives,* Pluto Press, 1983, p.87.

42 Flannery, Gregory, "Military rape, the ugly secret in the American armed forces", *City Beat,* vol 8, issue 41, 22 August 2002.

43 *Prosecutor v. Jean-Paul Akayesu,* Case No. ICTR-96-4-T, Judgment of 2 September 1998.

44 See *Sudan: Darfur: Rape as a weapon of war – sexual violence and its consequences* (AI Index: AFR 54/076/2004).

45 *Peru: The Truth and Reconciliation Commission – a first step towards a country without injustice* (AI Index: AMR 46/003/2004).

46 Article 15-6 Investigation of the 800th Military Police Brigade (The Taguba Report), Findings and recommendations, section 7 (k), cited in Miles, Steven, "Abu Ghraib: its legacy for military medicine", *The Lancet,* Vol. 364, No. 9435, 21 August 2004.

47 The mass rapes of Bangladeshi women were a key example in Brownmiller, Susan, *Against Our Will: Men, Women and Rape,* Simon and Schuster, 1975.

48 *Report of the Special Rapporteur on violence against women, its causes and consequences, mission to Rwanda,* UN Doc. E/CN.4/1998/54/Add.1, 1997.

49 The right to the highest attainable standard of health is codified in a variety of international and regional instruments: Universal Declaration of Human Rights, Article 25; International Covenant on Economic, Social and Cultural Rights, Article 12; Convention on the Elimination of All Forms of Discrimination against Women, Article 12; Convention on the Rights of the Child, Article 24; African Charter on Human and Peoples' Rights, Article 16; African Charter on the Rights and Welfare of the Child, Article 14; Protocol to the African Charter on the Rights of Women in Africa, Article 14; Additional Protocol to the American Convention on Human Rights in the Area of Economic, Social and Cultural Rights "Protocol of San Salvador", Article 10; European Social Charter, Article 11.

50 General Comment 14 on the Right to the highest attainable standard of health, UN Committee on Economic, Social and Cultural Rights, UN Doc. E/C.12/2000/4, 2000.

51 Rehn, Elisabeth and Sirleaf, Ellen Johnson, *Women, War, Peace: The Independent Experts' Assessment of the Impact of Armed Conflict on Women and Women's Role in Peace-building,* UNIFEM, 2002, p.41.

52 *Liberia: One year after Accra – immense human rights challenges remain* (AI Index: AFR 34/012/2004) p. 6.

53 *Liberia: The promises of peace for 21,000 child soldiers* (AI Index: AFR 34/006/2004).

54 *2002 FAO State of Food Insecurity*, cited in *Marked for Death - Rape Survivors Living with HIV/AIDS in Rwanda* (AI Index: AFR 47/007/2004), p.4.

55 *Report of the Secretary-General to the Security Council on the protection of civilians in armed conflict*, UN Doc. S/1999/957, 1999.

56 Beijing Platform for Action.

57 *Política Nacional De Salud Sexual Y Reproductiva*, Ministerio De Protección Social, 2003, p.14, cited in *Colombia: "Scarred bodies, hidden crimes" – Sexual violence against women in the armed conflict* (AI Index: AMR 23/040/2004).

58 One of the five commitments made to refugee women by the UN High Commissioner for Refugees in 2001 was that UNHCR would provide individual registration and relevant documentation to all refugee women in order to ensure their individual security, freedom of movement and access to essential services. This commitment, however, remains unimplemented in several refugee settings around the world.

59 *UNHCR Policy on Refugee Women and Guidelines on their Protection - An Assessment of 10 Years of their Implementation, An Independent Assessment*, Women's Commission for Refugee Women and Children, May 2002, p.35.

60 Rajasingham-Senanayake, Dharini, "Ambivalent Empowerment: The Tragedy of Tamil Women in Conflict", in Manchanda, Rita, ed., *Women, War and Peace in South Asia*, Sage New Delhi, 2001, p.102.

61 *Women, Peace and Security, Study submitted to Secretary-General pursuant to Security Council resolution 1325 (2000)*, United Nations Publication, 2002, p.26.

62 *World Report 1999*, Human Rights Watch, 1999.

63 Report of the High Commissioner for Human Rights on Systematic Rape, Sexual Slavery and Slavery-like Practices During Armed Conflict, UN Doc. E/CN.4/Sub.2/2002/28.

64 Rehn, Elisabeth and Sirleaf, Ellen Johnson, *Women, War, Peace: The Independent Experts' Assessment of the Impact of Armed Conflict on Women and Women's Role in Peace-building*, UNIFEM, 2002, p.26.

65 Rehn, Elisabeth and Sirleaf, Ellen Johnson, *Women, War, Peace: The Independent Experts' Assessment of the Impact of Armed Conflict on Women and Women's Role in Peace-building*, UNIFEM, 2002, p.26.

66 *UN Secretary-General's Bulletin, Special measures for protection from sexual exploitation and sexual abuse*, UN Doc. ST/SGB/2003/13.

67 *Note for Implementing and Operational Partners by UNHCR and Save the Children-UK on Sexual Violence & Exploitation: The Experience of Refugee Children in Guinea, Liberia and Sierra Leone based on Initial Findings and Recommendations from Assessment Mission, 22 October-30 November 2001*, February 2002.

68 *Forgotten Children of War – Sierra Leonean refugee children in Guinea*, Human Rights Watch, 1999.

69 Presentation to Amnesty International by Felicity Hill, UNIFEM, March 2004.

70 *UNHCR Policy on Refugee Women and Guidelines on their Protection – An Assessment of 10 Years of their Implementation, An Independent Assessment*, Women's Commission for Refugee Women and Children, May 2002, p.11.

71 *Israel and the Occupied Territories: Surviving under siege – The impact of movement restrictions on the right to work* (AI Index: MDE 15/001/2003).

72 *Women in the front line: human rights violations against women* (AI Index: ACT 77/001/1991), p.29.

73 *Final Report of the Commission of Inquiry into Involuntary Removal or Disappearance of Persons*, Sri Lanka Sessional Papers, 1997, p.127.

74 Zur, Judith, *Violent Memories: Maya War Widows in Guatemala*, Westview Press, 1998, pp.127-128.

75 *Laos: Military atrocities against Hmong children are war crimes* (AI Index: ASA 26/004/2004).

76 *Reproductive health during conflict and displacement*, World Health Organization, 2000.

77 McKay, Susan and Mazurana, Dyan, *Girls in Militaries, Paramilitaries, and Armed Opposition Groups*, Department of Foreign Affairs and International Trade, 2001, p.7.

78 UN Development Programme, *Human Development Report*, 1995, p.45.

79 "Confronting Rape in the Military", *New York Times*, 12 March 2004.

80 *Colombia: "Scarred bodies, hidden crimes" – Sexual violence against women in the armed conflict* (AI Index: AMR 23/040/2004).

81 Report of The Special Rapporteur on Violence Against Women, its causes and consequences, *Integration of the Human Rights of Women and the Gender Perspective – Mission to Colombia*, 2002, UN Doc. E/N.4/2002/83/Add.3.

82 McKay, Susan and Mazurana, Dyan, *Girls in Militaries, Paramilitaries, and Armed Opposition Groups*, Department of Foreign Affairs and International Trade, 2001, p.5.

83 Alfredson, Lisa, *Sexual Exploitation Of Child Soldiers: an exploration and analysis of global dimensions and trends*, Coalition to Stop the Use of Child Soldiers, December 2001, p.5.

84 Keairns, Yvonne E., *Voices of Girl Soldiers Summary Report*, Quaker UN Offices, 2002, p.7.

85 *Liberia: The promises of peace for 21,000 child soldiers* (AI Index: AFR 34/006/2004), p.4, and *Sierra Leone: Childhood – a casualty of conflict* (AI Index: AFR 51/069/2000).

86 *Off Target: The Conduct of the War and Civilian Casualties in Iraq*, Human Rights Watch, 2003.

87 Davies, P, *War of the Mines: Cambodia, landmines and the impoverishment of a nation*, Pluto Press, 1994, pp.21-22.

88 Colburn, Marta, *Gender and Development in Yemen*, 2001, Oxfam GB and Friedrich-Erich-Stiftung, p.171.

89 *Shattered Lives – the case for tough international arms controls*, Amnesty International and Oxfam (AI Index: ACT 30/001/2003).

90 *Shattered Lives – the case for tough international arms controls*, Amnesty International and Oxfam (AI Index: ACT 30/001/2003).

91 *Rwanda: "Marked for Death" – rape survivors living with HIV/AIDS in Rwanda* (AI Index: AFR 47/007/2004), p.3, fn 2 and p.3.

92 See, for example the *Barrios Altos* case, *Inter-American Commission on Human Rights v Peru*, judgement of 14 March 2001, Inter-Am Ct. H.R. (Ser. C) No. 75.

93 *Universal jurisdiction: the duty of states to enact and implement legislation* (AI Index: IOR 53/002-018/2001).

94 Committee on the Elimination of Discrimination against Women, General Recommendation 19, Violence against women, 1992, UN Doc. HRI\GEN\1\Rev.1.

95 UN Declaration on the Elimination of Violence against Women, UN Doc. A/RES/48/104, adopted by the UN General Assembly on 20 December 1993.

96 *Report of the Special Rapporteur on Violence against Women, Violence against Women perpetrated and/or condoned by the State during times of armed conflict* (1997-2000), 2001, UN Doc. E/CN.4/2001/73; *Report of the Special Rapporteur on Violence against Women, Towards an effective implementation of international norms to end violence against women*, 2003, UN Doc. E/CN.4/2004/66.

97 Charlesworth, H. and Chinkin, C., *The Boundaries of International Law: A Feminist Analysis*, Manchester University Press, 2000, pp.314-5.

98 *Prosecutor v. Jean-Paul Akayesu*, Case No. ICTR-96-4-T, Judgment of 2 September 1998.

99 *Prosecutor v. Kunarać et al*, Case No. IT-96-23 and IT-96-23/1, Trial Chamber II, Judgment of 22 February 2001.

100 *Prosecutor v. Kunarać et al*, Case No. IT-96-23 and IT-96-23/1, Trial Chamber II, Judgment of 22 February 2001.

101 In one case, *Prosecutor v. Tadić*, it permitted the use of anonymous witnesses, which Amnesty International opposes, see *International Criminal Court: Making the right choices – Part II: Organizing the court and ensuring a fair trial* (AI Index: IOR 40/011/1997).

102 *Akayesu* judgment, para 598.

103 The *Akayesu* definition of rape, although hailed as a significant advance in 1998, is in some ways more restrictive than the more recent jurisprudence of the International Criminal Tribunal for the former Yugoslavia in the *Kunarać* case (Case No. IT-96-23, Judgment, Appeals Chamber, 12 June 2002).

104 Now renamed Women's Initiatives for Gender Justice, see: www.iccwomen.org.

105 These include the 1996 Draft Codes of Crimes against the Peace and Security of Mankind adopted by the International Law Commission.

106 Article 36(8)(a)(iii) of the Rome Statute of the International Criminal Court.

107 As of 11 October 2004.

108 Amnesty International on 21 September 2004 applied to submit an *amicus curiae* petition to the Nigerian Federal High Court, demonstrating that the decision by the Nigerian Government to grant refugee status to Charles Taylor with apparent guarantees to protect him from prosecution for crimes against humanity and war crimes violates Nigeria's obligations under international law. See *Nigeria: Amicus Curiae brief submitted to the Federal High Court reviewing refugee status granted to Charles Taylor* (AI Index: AFR 44/030/2004).

109 *International Criminal Court: US efforts to obtain impunity for genocide, crimes against humanity and war crimes* (AI Index: IOR 40/025/2002).

110 See, for example, *Afghanistan: 'no one listens to us and no one treats us as human beings' – Justice denied to women* (AI Index: ASA 11/023/2003).

111 Farr, Vanessa, "Information, Data and Statistics" from *Women in an Insecure World*, Geneva Centre for the Democratic Control of Armed Forces, p. 147.

112 *Rwanda: "Marked for Death" – Rape Survivors Living with HIV/AIDS in Rwanda* (AI Index: AFR 47/007/2004).

113 See *Senegal: Casamance Women Speak Out* (AI Index: AFR 49/002/2003).

114 See website: www1.jca.apc.org/vaww-net-japan/english/womenstribunal2000/basicpapers. html.

115 *Peru: The Truth and Reconciliation Commission – a first step towards a country without injustice* (AI Index: AMR 46/003/2004).

116 *Women, Peace and Security, Study submitted by the Secretary-General pursuant to Security Council resolution 1325 (2000)*, United Nations Publication, 2002.

117 Rehn, Elisabeth and Sirleaf, Ellen Johnson, *Women, War, Peace: The Independent Experts' Assessment of the Impact of Armed Conflict on Women and Women's Role in Peace-building*, UNIFEM, 2002.

118 *Women, Peace and Security, Study submitted by the Secretary-General pursuant to Security Council resolution 1325 (2000)*, United Nations Publication, 2002.

119 Testimony given to Amnesty International in September 2003.

120 *Fourth progress report of the Secretary-General on the United Nations Mission in Liberia*, UN Doc. S/2004/725, 10 September 2004, para 17.

121 The Joint United Nations Programme on HIV/AIDS.

122 See for example, *Sudan: Surviving Rape in Darfur* (AI Index: AFR 54/097/2004); *Kosovo (Serbia and Montenegro): "So does it mean that we have the rights?" Protecting the human rights of women and girls trafficked for*

forced prostitution in Kosovo (AI Index: EUR 70/010/2004); *Burundi: Rape – the hidden human rights abuse* (AI Index: AFR 16/006/2004); *Afghanistan: "No one listens to us and no one treats us as human beings" – Justice denied to women* (AI Index: ASA 11/023/2003); *Iraq: Human rights protection and promotion vital in the transitional period* (AI Index: MDE 14/030/2004); *Russian Federation: Chechen Republic:"Normalization" in whose eyes?* (AI Index: EUR 46/027/2004); *Haiti: Breaking the cycle of violence – A last chance for Haiti?* (AI Index: AMR 36/038/2004); *Colombia: "Scarred bodies, hidden crimes" – Sexual violence against women and the armed conflict* (AI Index: AMR 23/040/2004).

123 *Final Report of the Commission of Experts Established Pursuant to Security Council Resolution 780 (1992),* UN Doc. S/1994/674, 27 May 1994. "The reported cases of rape and sexual assault contained in the database occurred between the fall of 1991 and the end of 1993. The majority of the rapes occurred from April to November 1992; fewer occurred in the following five months. In the same time period, the number of media reports increased from a few in March 1992 to a high of 535 news stories in January 1993 and 529 in February 1993. This correlation could indicate that the media attention caused the decline. In that case, it would indicate that commanders could control the alleged perpetrators if they wanted to. This could lead to the conclusion that there was an overriding policy advocating the use of rape as a method of 'ethnic cleansing', rather than a policy of omission, tolerating the widespread commission of rape."

124 Susanne Schmeidl with Eugenia Piza-López, "Gender and Conflict Early Warning: A Preliminary Framework," Swiss Peace Foundation and International Alert, 2002.

125 The UN Declaration on the Elimination of Violence against Women defines the term "violence against women" as "any act of gender-based violence that results in, or is likely to result in, physical, sexual or psychological harm or suffering to women, including threats of such acts, coercion or arbitrary deprivation of liberty, whether occurring in public or in private life." (Article 1) Gender-based violence is violence that is directed against a woman because she is a woman or that affects women disproportionately.

126 In this chapter, Amnesty International uses the term "women" to include women of all ages, including girls.

127 CEDAW General Recommendation 19, para 16.